**WALTER
VAN BEIRENDONCK
CUT
THE WORLD
AWAKE**

XXX Walter

For Dirk,
XXX Walter

WALTER VAN BEIRENDONCK

CUT THE WORLD AWAKE

HANNIBAL

A WORD FROM WALTER

CUT THE WORLD AWAKE and *DRAW THE WORLD AWAKE*
are two books like no other. I'm exposing never-before-seen layers
of my methodology as a fashion designer.

I treat every collection like an adventure.
A hunt/search for exactly what I want to say and how I want to say it.
For the past four decades, and to the present day, with no plans to stop,
twice a year, I go on such a quest.

The journey always has a clear, very private beginning: my collages.
Then, after taking several other meticulous leaps, a breathtaking public climax follows:
my runway shows in Paris.

But the process always starts with me physically sitting down and cutting out images and
words. Of course, in between collections I never stop dreaming, looking, fantasising.
But it's not until I take out a brand-new blank-paged, black-covered book,
a stack of magazines and printouts, sharp scissors and a thick glue stick that the swirls
in my mind start taking some sort of form.

Art is about honest confrontation.
Not only with the world around you, but equally within yourself.
It's also about juxtaposing specific elements that move and inspire you against each other.
See how they interact. Do they play nicely? Or is a fascinating clash forming?
Can I see shapes emerging? Colours that excite me?

If that sounds abstract, that's because it is.
Nothing is crystal clear at this point in my process, but little by little,
thoughts and ideas, once foggy, start coming into focus.

I have always preferred a direct approach to living and storytelling.
But to create honest, multi-layered work that stands the test of time,
you must be willing to explore multiple levels.
This requires courage and unwavering focus,
and it's these strengths that I bring to my creative process.

What I have learnt is that, in the end, with the clothes and other work I put out,
I can ride the volume. I can turn it up, I can whisper but still in a Walter way.
Reveal what I want to reveal. But not with my collages.
With my collages, I am as unnuanced, graphic and explicit as I want to be.

When it comes to shocking and provoking the world awake,
I've found a kindred spirit in the great artist and my hero Paul McCarthy,
with whom I got to have a big conversation for this book.

My wish for each of you is that you don't treat *CUT THE WORLD AWAKE* as
a one-way experience, from me to you, but that you set out to make your own
inner and outer connections with the universe at large.

Figure out your own steps and find your voice, the stories you want to tell.
Whether it's by cutting, drawing, downloading, doing, writing, talking, designing, connecting…

Now go and slice away the unnecessary,
dream up new hybrids and enjoy the magic!

XXX

WALTER

CUT THE WORLD AWAKE

**A conversation between
Walter Van Beirendonck & Dominique Nzeyimana**

DOMINIQUE NZEYIMANA: I consider all our interviews a long continuous conversation, but this one in particular follows our extensive dialogue published in *DRAW THE WORLD AWAKE*. So, for a fuller picture, readers should pick up that incredible book as well. It's such a monumental piece of work. While *DRAW THE WORLD AWAKE* showcases your incredible drawings, *CUT THE WORLD AWAKE* is a selection of the collages you create and use as inspiration or as a pre-study for your design process.

WALTER VAN BEIRENDONCK: "The collages happen before I start drawing. It's the moment when I'm mainly in my head. I'm thinking, looking at things, researching, reading books, Googling images, studying photographs, going to exhibitions... A combination of all those things, really. I'm absorbing all these impressions, and then suddenly I'm done and I want to put these morphed thoughts to paper to confront them, almost. What's important to me in this process is to create some kind of clash. That way, I come to a result or conclusion of sorts. It can be a decision about an atmosphere or can purely revolve around shapes or a colour scheme. In fact, I use my collages to put things to paper physically and to synthesise all that's in my mind or at least make a deliberate move towards the next step, which is drawing my looks."

Do you know what you're looking for before you start cutting?

WVB: "No, it's very random. Sometimes I only use images that I cut out of magazines, and sometimes I use print-outs because the difference in quality or sharpness is closer to the tone I'm looking for. Then I start putting pictures and words together to create a certain mood. It all happens very haphazardly, very freely. But all the while keeping a goal in mind, of course. I know that I want to capture a certain spirit and glue to paper what interests me at that very moment. I know whether I want to go for a more extreme, aggressive, subdued or a more dreamy, fairy-tale-like approach."

Do you mainly source from your private library or do you go out to find different magazines? What is the gathering process like?

WVB: "I have boxes stuffed with clippings."

You collect these throughout the year?

WVB: "I have loads of publications that I set aside during the year and I'm not afraid to cut into them. Which ends disastrously for some magazines, but so be it. I don't purposefully seek out certain titles. I know which are more suited than others ——— they're mostly culture-focused magazines with clear and striking imagery. I don't pick out those with tiny photos, so a lot of Japanese magazines are unfortunately not suitable for collages. But they don't have to be fashion magazines per se. Then, I start fantasising and cutting into them. Sometimes the collages are purely made out of the contrasts between texts or words. Other times it's more about a certain mood, or silhouette, a hairdo or make-up look. It depends."

The collages are more raw than your drawings. Not specifically when it comes to the execution, because they become new art pieces in and of themselves, but more so in terms of emotion. They are more straightforward.

WVB: "Yes, because that's just easier to achieve through collage. In designing the clothing it all gets a bit smoothed out. But I do think that the undertone of my collections is decided then and there, through collaging and the context I want to infuse into those collages. Then you get the next phase: the drawings interpreting the collages. Only then does the development towards the collections start. That's how I go from more raw to polished."

In terms of the kind of emotions you put to paper... All those layers are somehow felt in the collection, but not as overtly. It's very nuanced and that is beautiful to me, that kind of distilling.

WVB: "The early inspiration is tangible and I can play with the volume any way I want. Or even afterwards, I decide how much I want to divulge or maybe only talk about in certain conversations or with the press. For *I HAVE SEEN THE FUTURE...*, the latest collection before this book went to print, the subtext was very intense but few people can pinpoint it. Most of the audience just sees circus and clowns and thinks: happy feelings. That's fine, the underlying influences don't need to be obvious."

In this book, your love for the arts is clearly visible. You told me you experimented with visual art and art installations while you were a student.

WVB: "And now you want to hear that story *again*?" (*laughs*)

I have said it before, your stories never get old and I think this is a rather obscure one that I want to get on record. As a bonus, it features Dirk before you were a couple.

WVB: "This was early on during my time in Antwerp. There was a space in Antwerp called 'Today's Place' that was very much about art performances. A group of students from the Royal Academy of Fine Arts, from the painting department who I knew through Narcisse Tordoir, put it all together. They asked me to do a performance and, at first, I didn't feel up to it. I didn't consider myself to be an artist at all then. I had just started studying fashion and I was also taking photography evening classes along with Martin Margiela. I had the idea of making a series of self-portraits, posing with a mixture of skinned dead rabbits and rabbits that were very much alive. The name of the performance was 'Red Rabbit Virility'. I made a bunch of slides and I showed them at Today's Place one night, during an exhibition or an evening of performances. Mine were slightly gloomy images with a lot of reds and red light. I still have all of them. I'm holding rabbits in some of them and I wasn't wearing a lot of clothes either. It was rather abstract and had more of a performance feel. I took the photos myself. We had a paint-spraying booth at home so I took the photos there, with a self-timer, holding multiple rabbits. Then, when I went to buy the skinned one at a poulterer's in the De Wilde Zee neighbourhood, I ran into Dirk. We weren't a couple then. That happened later. But of course it was weird! I had to explain why I was running around town with a dead bunny."

After that performance, did you quickly pick up on the fact that photography or visual arts was not your path?

WVB: "Back then I was exploring, and it became clear quite soon that fashion was my real calling. I was obsessed with everything about David Bowie and what he was doing looks-wise. I wanted to pursue that."

Over the years, you have also organised and designed a lot of exhibitions —— which I feel is one of your great strengths. When you look at the more artistic side of Walter Van Beirendonck, which of those moments stand out most to you?

WVB: "One of the most important projects as a curator was *FASHION 2001 LANDED–GELAND*."

I think that city-wide installation was a shift for a lot of art and fashion lovers here in Belgium.

WVB: "For me, it coincided with the brutal break from Mustang and Wild & Lethal Trash and going back to working completely independently. An important moment. After quitting W.&L.T. I had to find a way to reinvigorate myself. I got an incredible opportunity from the city of Antwerp where they just handed me a budget for a two-year project and I got 'carte blanche'. I remember the joy of shouldering that project, doing the research, proposing all the ideas. At first, I was just the overseeing curator and I had meant to appoint other people to execute the exhibitions, but that part fell through."

Did it fall through because no one was able to execute your vision independently?

WVB: "I honestly spoke to many candidates and had serious sit-downs but they would always come at it from certain specific worlds: the classical arts, modern arts, ethnic arts, but it felt like no one dared merge everything together. I knew I had to take the reins to make it work. For instance, the *MUTILATE?* exhibition at M HKA. I made some very radical decisions there, had some pretty extraordinary installations made and touched on a theme that is very important in fashion: the theme of mutilation. It was a very powerful fashion exhibition, on how fashion thinks and operates. It felt like a huge playground. As a curator, I think that was really important for me, making certain statements, like *2WOMEN* on Gabrielle Chanel and Rei Kawakubo. The fact that Rei allowed those five shows to take place and allowed me to do the styling for the collections myself. She never lets that happen! It was about creating energy within a city. It was so unique and unheard of. But perhaps if I could have done this in a larger city than Antwerp, it could have been that big whirlwind that drew in the entire world to see."

Just as in *MUTILATE?* in your collages, it's a returning motif to see your view on beauty —— which you have always unabashedly pushed forward.

WVB: "Diversity was always very normal to me. I think 1995 was a good example of that, the *TWINKLE, TWINKLE, LITTLE STAR* show I did at Felix Pakhuis. It was boys, girls, different ethnicities, tall, short, big or thin. My dog Sado was part of it, or a stand-in white bull terrier was. Sometimes certain collections are more able to be inclusive than others. I've always been very interested in the fluidity of different types and I've embraced that —— but I also don't have to do it in a desperate way."

In the early days, there was a time when your work was a bit misunderstood. Now, it really seems like a great time to put your collages out there. If you had published this book 20 years ago, the majority would've remained stuck on the more explicit images:

"Walter is angry, controversial, overly sexual." Do you feel that too: this great momentum of putting an overview out there?

WVB: "Absolutely —— I feel that with DRAW THE WORLD AWAKE too. I think now is the right time because I have done a lot of work and there is a lot to show. You're not getting judged on one collection but an entire body of work. It's the same with the collages. Some things can get misinterpreted —— they still might be. By bringing them all together, you can see that the work goes in all directions. For my exhibition DREAM THE WORLD AWAKE at MoMu Antwerp, things also went from LET'S TELL A FAIRYTALE to S&M in a very organic way, and that's how it all flows in my mind as well. And I have more ideas for the future that reveal my way of working —— subverting the fashion world and being a 'terrorist' in this scene. It's a fact that even when looking at older collections, I was never really affirming what was going on in the fashion world at the time."

It was relating to what was happening in the world at large and a lot of those things were being blatantly ignored by the fashion industry: AIDS, racism, war, pollution…

WVB: "That continues to be the case, really. It's still a bit 'not done' to approach the fashion world in the way that I do."

I want to emphasise the moment we're in now —— and what people will look back on in later years, wondering what it was like. You're the last one of the Antwerp Six+1 still standing. Everyone has retired or has chosen to step away from their creative director positions. A few weeks ago, you went to Dries Van Noten's final show, at a time when your own output at Paris Fashion Week was multiple and on such a high. What's your take on this juncture?

WVB: "I'm having very contrasting feelings. I can understand why my peers have taken a step back from their own brand, each for their own reasons. There might have been an overwhelming urge to cash in. And that is not disrespectful, because no matter how you look at it, all of them did. I get it, it provides a certain sense of security. But I don't feel like I'd be able to, because my label is structured differently, because my way of working is pretty unique. Of course, to be on somewhat of a career high and to be the last one standing feels both extraordinary and weird. But these are all important stages. I feel like I am very sharp and have stayed relevant, so that gives me the drive to keep going. There's enough motivation left. I don't really feel like I need to close a chapter. Being in Paris, I could tell how much young people are still interested in my work. A twenty-year-old girl walked into the gallery and bought one of my drawings. She had worn my clothing since childhood and buying my artwork was a natural evolution for her. I was approached in the street by a group of young Black designers who had come all the way from Ghana to Paris to showcase their collection. They were beautiful guys, dressed in their own brand and they told me what my work meant to them. Moments like that give you enormous satisfaction. It makes me feel like I'm still doing well. Why would I stop when I'm still swinging?"* (*laughs*)

*note: in reference to David Bowie's 'Boys Keep Swinging'.

WALTER VAN BEIRENDONCK'S BIG DREAM CONVERSATION WITH PAUL McCARTHY

PAUL McCARTHY, c.1953

WALTER VAN BEIRENDONCK, c.1961

PAUL McCARTHY:
(*pops onto screen*) "Hey, am I here?"

WALTER VAN BEIRENDONCK:
Yes, hello!

PMC: (*laughs*) "How are you?"

WVB: Good! I fondly remember when I visited you in LA, and you gave me and my friends a tour of your studio. I will be releasing two books that showcase my preparatory work as a fashion designer. The one in which this talk will be featured focuses on the collages that I make. And it is because you and your work have been so important to me and my evolution as a fashion designer that it was a dream for me to have a conversation in this book, so I can explain what you have meant to me. I want to introduce Dominique; she does all the writing for both *DRAW THE WORLD AWAKE* and *CUT THE WORLD AWAKE*, so she will work on the interview.

DOMINIQUE NZEYIMANA: Yes, I will. Walter and I looked for the topics you both have in common and that have fascinated you over the past decade. That's what he'll be talking to you about. Paul, if you have any questions for Walter while this conversation is ongoing, please ask them. I think it's really great that Dylan (*Paul McCarthy's longtime studio manager, ed. note*) has just turned off his camera. I will do the same so both of you can just converse. It's better that the two of you have a talk. It's so nice to meet you and thank you for being here. Is this early for you?"

PMC: "No, no, no, it's not. I usually get up pretty early. I go to bed really late and get up pretty early."

WVB: Dominique, before you turn off your camera, maybe you can show Paul *DRAW THE WORLD AWAKE*?

(Dominique holds up the baby-blue-covered 960-pages-and-counting *DRAW THE WORLD AWAKE* book to the camera. Showing all sides and some pages to Paul McCarthy.)

WVB: Paul, we worked on two books; this is the first one we've just completed. It's a book with all my sketches, a big selection of the drawings for my collections. I've been working this way since the beginning. I make all my drawings first, and only then do I start to make the collections. These are not illustrations; they are essential work tools, making them very special to me. After this book there will be a second one, with a baby-pink cover, giving an overview of my collages. That's where this talk will be printed.

My first encounter with your work was during the early 90s. I saw the installation and video from 'Heidi,' the collaborative work with Mike Kelley at Centre Pompidou in Paris. Seeing this blew my mind wide open, and it made me realise that art with strong and provocative messages could also be funny and colourful, an approach that was so different and new at that time. I was extremely shocked. It opened my eyes and allowed me to introduce harsh themes and explicit graphics in my fashion work but in a 'lighter way'. Thinking back to the 'Heidi' installation, what was that process like for you?

PMC: "The process for 'Heidi' had been going on for a long time before that showing. In the 70s, I don't know, probably towards the end of the 70s, I had done performances, and I had used rubber masks that I would buy at different stores on Hollywood Boulevard. I was always shopping on Hollywood Boulevard. It's not the Hollywood you think of now. There would be these kind of costume stores and gag shops, and I would just go there and buy a rubber mask. It was probably in '73 I bought the first rubber masks. I had been making work involving some form of disguise, using a mask or covering my face. That had been ongoing. At some point in the late 70s, I was already appropriating subjects, I started thinking about appropriating a film of some sort. I came up with Heidi and Popeye, then. I wrote the script to do 'Heidi' in the late 70s. I had gotten an exchange grant in France and I asked if I could do the project in the French Alps. I wanted to do it outdoors. Years passed, and they cancelled the exchange but still gave me the money. Since the exchange didn't happen, 'Heidi' didn't happen. Years later, I was invited to do this project in Vienna, a group show of LA artists. I said I wanted to make 'Heidi'. At the same time, Mike Kelley and I wanted to do something together. We decided to collaborate and Mike was going to do a project in Vienna around Adolf Loos, the architect. So, we combined these two subjects. Adolf Loos and the American Bar and his Modernist philosophy and then this Heidi chalet. I still wanted to do it outdoors, but it was impossible, so we filmed everything inside the gallery. One of the things I'm working on now is making another 'Heidi'."

WVB: (*hums approvingly*).

PMC: "I think I understood it back then, but I didn't really go deep into the subject because it was a collaboration. I pushed the issues I was interested in, and Mike was also interested in them, but I want to explore them further. If a new Heidi actually happens, I don't know... (*Looks to the side*) There's a box over there that's about making 'Heidi'."

WVB: So during that time, I was working on my collection *KILLER / ASTRAL TRAVELLER / 4D-Hi-D*. I wanted to talk about the AIDS epidemic, which was a huge issue back then. While working on prints, I introduced Heidi alongside the Goat, symbolising both the devil and that terrible disease. I was also fascinated by 'cultural gothic'. So, it allowed me to go rather deep into subjects that were not talked about in the fashion world at that time. You helped me find my own language and add more depth to my collections. Up until then, for some people, I was the designer with the funny, colourful T-shirts and prints, but from then on, if you looked beyond the surface, you would discover so much more storytelling and catch the contemporary subjects that fascinated me.

PMC: "Oh, yeah, yeah."

WVB: Another inspiration we have in common is fairy tales. My second collection was called *LET'S TELL A FAIRYTALE*. When I started looking into your work years later, I met so many unforgettable characters showcasing your amazing fantasy, but they always contained these intense sexual and violent ingredients. I became so enthralled by these figures you were creating. For example, 'Tomato Head' is one of my favourite sculptures you have created, 'Spaghetti Man', too. All these kinds of characters really spoke to my imagination. I think you might know about this, but I curated an exhibition in Rotterdam named 'POWERMASK' and we had 'Spaghetti Man' as one of the main sculptures. It was fantastic for me to have it included in an environment I created. We both have this fairy-tale, Santa Claus feeling about us. People are always comparing me to Santa Claus with the beard. It's nice to feel that connection with you.

PMC: "Santa Claus, yes. My beard comes and goes, since I was about 16 or 17 I've had a beard. I grow a beard and then it goes away for a few months. There was a period in the 70s for four or five years when I didn't have a beard, but I've otherwise had a beard. It disappears depending on what character I'm working on. The last few years, I have been cutting the beard off for videos that I've been working on. In 'White Snow' I was Walt Disney, in 'DADDA', Donald Trump. I'm Max in 'Night Vater', and then Adolf Hitler in 'A&E', (*laughs*) but basically I'm lazy and don't want to shave."

WVB: A mixture because they're not all fantasy figures.

PMC: "I would go four or five months between characters and grow a beard. During that whole time, like the 'Heidi' project, I'm kind of back in that space. I have a new Santa Claus project I've been wanting to do for a while. So, each time I grew the beard in between the projects, I thought: 'Okay, now I'll do the Santa project.' I've put it off. Like the 'Heidi' one, but I'm returning to these characters again."

WVB: The ones you did before.

PMC: "'Heidi' is all about the grandfather, and I'm older now; I'm a grandfather in real life. I've always wanted to play the grandfather, and then after that I can play the Santa Claus too. These characters, they're hanging in there."

WVB: When I first grew my beard in the 90s, people reacted very strangely to me. At that time, it was not done for a fashion designer, so it was also rather weird that by just growing a beard, you were making a statement. I feel that so much in your work, that you don't compromise and that you go for complete and utter freedom. That's something that's so precious, the fact that you just go for it and that you found your voice without compromising very early on.

PMC: "I don't know. (*thinks*) When I made 'Heidi' with Mike, I have a lot of fondness for that period in time, the late 80s. Before 'Heidi', in the 70s, there were these performances like 'Sailor's Meat' and the 'Black/White Tapes'. I wasn't thinking about galleries ——— not even considering galleries or money, or an art world career. During that period, the performances in art were much darker. I didn't make as much work in the 80s because we had kids and we were living quite poor. We had no money. I was struggling just to work and have a job and all this kind of stuff. I made a lot of drawings but I quit doing performances. The sculptures like 'Spaghetti Man' were all coming a lot later. It wasn't until the 90s that I first sold any work. That's when these sorts of fabrications all happened, things like 'Spaghetti Man' and 'Tomato Head'. And in a way, those pieces like 'Heidi' ——— which was in the late 80s?"

WVB: I discovered it in '92, '93.

PMC: "I made 'Heidi' in the 80s, I guess? I'm not sure when I made it. I made 'Family Tyranny' in the 80s, in '87, so it was after that. That period of the 90s was about trying to adjust. (*thinks*) In each one of these ten-year periods, how I existed as an artist changed. In the 90s, I started teaching, which meant I had some money, and now I'm adjusting to what that all means. I got a gallery and became an artist with some form of influence and means. Also with teaching, I experimented. There was still the whole thing of figuration, but I think that period, which lasted

PAUL McCARTHY and MIKE KELLEY
Heidi, Midlife Crisis Trauma Center and Negative Media-Engram Abreaction Release Zone, 1992
Performance, video, photographs, installation

© Paul McCarthy and Mike Kelley Foundation for the Arts.
Courtesy the artists and Hauser & Wirth.

PAUL McCARTHY
Tomato Head (Black), 1994
Fiberglass, urethane, rubber, metal, clothing (62 objects)
213.4 × 139.7 × 11.7 cm

© Paul McCarthy. Courtesy the artist and Hauser & Wirth.
Photo: Douglas Parker

PAUL McCARTHY
Spaghetti Man, 1993
Fiberglass, metal, urethane, rubber, acrylic fur, clothing
254 × 84 × 56 cm
Penis length 1.270 cm
© Paul McCarthy. Courtesy the artist and Hauser & Wirth.

PAUL McCARTHY
WS White Snow Mammoth, 2013
Performance, video, photographic series

© Paul McCarthy. Courtesy the artist and Hauser & Wirth.
Photo: Louisa McCarthy

PAUL McCARTHY
WS White Snow, 2013
Performance, video, installation, photographs
Directed by Paul McCarthy and Damon McCarthy

© Paul McCarthy. Courtesy the artist and Hauser & Wirth.
Photo: Jeremiah McCarthy

PAUL McCARTHY
Tokyo Santa, 1996
Performance, video, b/w and colour photographs, drawings, installation
Tomio Koyama Gallery, Tokyo, Japan

© Paul McCarthy. Courtesy the artist and Hauser & Wirth.
Photo: Mitsuru Tanashi

PAUL McCARTHY
Santa Chocolate Shop, 1997
Performance, video, installation, colour photographs

© Paul McCarthy. Courtesy the artist and Hauser & Wirth.

PAUL McCARTHY
Tubbing, 1975
Performance, video, b/w and colour photographs

© Paul McCarthy. Courtesy the artist and Hauser & Wirth.
Photo: Al Payne

PAUL McCARTHY (with Mike Kelley)
Family Tyranny, 1987
Performance, video, and colour photographs

© Paul McCarthy. Courtesy the artist and Hauser & Wirth.
Photo: Steven Keller

PAUL McCARTHY (with Mike Kelley)
Cultural Soup, 1987
Video still
Single channel video, 6:59 min, colour, sound

© Paul McCarthy. Courtesy the artist and Hauser & Wirth.

from the 90s to the mid-2000s, is my period of 'the art world'. Teaching and being in the art world and the flow of money that came with that. I still believe in the pieces I made during that time, but the seduction of that world is also in there. I think, to a certain degree, what's going on now is a much darker situation. There is colour in there because I think I'm fascinated with certain types of colours, but the pieces I made the last few years are much darker and probably have fewer compromises. There's no compromising. The art world has changed an awful lot. I don't know about the fashion world, but I know within the art world artists have become subjects and workers to what the ultra-rich want."

WVB: That's also true in the fashion world, which has changed dramatically over the years. In my case, it was a rollercoaster of starting during the 80s in a similar situation: no money, trying to make it work, keeping on believing, doing a lot of commercial work and teaching as well. I started teaching at the Antwerp Fashion Department in 1985. It kept me going, I got paid and I could keep on believing. In the 90s, I worked with a company backing me, but in 2000 I made a total break. I chose to be fully independent, which I am to this day. It's an outsider position to be in, in the fashion world, which today is dominated by luxury houses and big companies that are spending and making so much money. I was also in that situation where I didn't want to compromise. I wanted to do my own thing, which definitely wasn't easy. But it's nice to hear that you're thinking in the same direction. Talking about teaching, you taught for a long time, no?

PMC: "I started teaching in 1985, too."

WVB: That's so funny that we started teaching the same year.

PMC: "I started teaching one class at UCLA as a kind of visiting teacher in 1985, but I started teaching full-time in 1990. It was a lucky circumstance. It was a situation of somebody that I knew getting into a position of being the head of a department and they would bring me in for one class. That had gone on a little bit before 1985. It was the same with Mike Kelley; we were brought in similarly. For a couple of years, we were brought in for one class or a three-week class. Chris Burden became head of the performance, video, and film department at UCLA, which was extraordinary that they hired him as head of a department. And he hired both Mike and me. Chris kept hiring me until they had to put me on full-time. It was an incredible thing. It took somebody like Chris getting into power..."

WVB: To have the guts to hire you.

PMC: "Otherwise, it wouldn't have happened. It's a really cool thing, so you also have to give credit to the person who hired Chris Burden."

WVB: My way of working as a teacher was to get into the heads of the students. Use my imagination to push them forward so they could explore and uncover their own talents. I wanted them to use their creativity to build a strong personal signature. I still miss the teaching and I am looking into new possibilities to pick it up again. Did you enjoy teaching?

PMC: "Yeah, it relieved the money problem to some degree. I was fixing people's toilets back then, taking whatever jobs I could get. At that time, artists in LA were teachers, that was a thing in California, in LA. I think it's directly related to CalArts and Allan Kaprow and John Baldessari. This idea of teaching as part of being an artist. It was a bit of a phenomenon. It's over now. Young, successful artists don't teach much."

WVB: They don't want to do it anymore? Or they don't need to?

PMC: "They have Art careers. It doesn't seem to be as much of a thing as it was before."

WVB: It's a good thing they have careers. It's the same in fashion. Young people are focused, from very early on, on being successful, creating the right portfolio to get into a big house, or working for a specific designer, and they're extremely ambitious. It's not about trial and error or experimenting, but about building a career from the beginning. Which is a big difference to the hit-or-miss period I started up in.

PMC: "I don't know, right now in LA, there are a lot of artists who are not part of the gallery systems or whose work doesn't fit the mould. A lot of performance, conceptual work that's really good. There are more of these sorts of artist collectives showing work in alternative spaces and other stuff like that. There's more of that right now than there has been in quite a while. I think that's because their work doesn't fit the galleries' or collectors' view of what art is."

WVB: Are they showing their work through social media?

PMC: "I think so. I've been making a lot of videos and quite a bit of AI lately. But I was thinking about what you've been doing and what your work is like, and what mine is about. And there's often this thing in my performance work that either I don't care what I have on when I'm doing something or I create a character of some sort. This thing of what does the character wear, what is he? How far do I take the character in terms of what they wear? What does Adolf Hitler wear, and what should I wear as an American pretending to be a buffoon-drunk Hitler? Of course, I'm not making a historical representation or period piece, so I'm not really looking for accuracy. Yes, there's a certain interest in: what kind of hat did Adolf Hitler wear? What kind of suit did Walt Disney wear? It sort of migrates. It's strange. In the characters where I was being Adolf Hitler, he, the character, started wearing Hawaiian shirts at some point. It's always strange; there are always coincidences that happen. I'm making these pieces, I'm wearing Hawaiian shirts and then, lo and behold, the boogaloo group of bigots appear wearing Hawaiian shirts. These cultural connections or coincidences… The thing of having an interest in what they wear and how far do I push or abstract it?"

WVB: Are you researching garments or clothes, or is it just in your imagination that you envision him wearing Hawaiian shirts? Is it more of a spontaneous thing that you try to do? Is it related to fashion or creating a look?

PMC: "It's been all of that."

WVB: Is it all coming from you? It's not that you're working with a stylist.

PMC: "I've never worked that way. I've thought about it sometimes, working with somebody on the clothes, but I never have. Sure, people who are around have given me input. Later, I'll think: 'Oh, I shouldn't have done that, that was the wrong decision'. And then I'll back off or go more extreme. But it's all part of the work. This thing of what they wear or what they don't wear, what the environment is, how do I abstract it? In your case, it seems that there's a point, the characters become like sculpture, they look like sculptures, it's kind of like the human body in a sculpture. I also get the sense that, in my case, the nose has always been a subject."

WVB: Why the nose? I saw the 'Pinocchio Pipenose Householddilemma' performance, in which you were walking around and pulling on garments, which was also centred around the nose. It was mesmerising to become part of your characters in this Pinocchio performance. I hold it close to my heart.

PMC: "The nose being phallic, the nose as a phallic symbol, on the face/brain, next to the brain like a 'dick brain', the obsession of the dick. It became like a mask. You change the nose, you change the face. But then, how far do I go with the nose? When you cross a certain line, you become something other, you become a cartoon or a character, a caricature. The range between human realism and the caricature or an abstraction. Caricature and distortion. Big head, big feet, big hands. You've made a caricature. You're saying: 'I am, at this point, outside of everyday life and as such, I am a form of language'. In these pieces I've been making lately, the line between somebody like Adolf Hitler or Donald Trump or Walt Disney, these kinds of archetypes or patriarchs in the form of cultural, societal vectors… To some degree, I stay close to the subject. The Hawaiian shirt is an everyday item, and these were all bought at thrift stores. I'm not abstracting it. The character I play looks fairly close to the actual person. I'm fairly good as a Disney character, pretty good as Trump and good as Hitler. I stay close to the subject. But by its very nature, there as an element of the other. My Adolf Hitler is a drunk American."

WVB: Funny to hear you talk about the Hawaiian shirt. It's a pattern I use from time to time. The typical Hawaiian flower says a lot. It's an excellent contrast in a silhouette. It gives the whole look another feeling and takes away the seriousness of the actual character. It projects a new exotic feeling, a new daring mood. It's nice to hear you notice the same things.

PMC: "You're on vacation. Hitler wearing a Hawaiian shirt is like he's on vacation."

WVB: He's on vacation, that's true.

PMC: "It's happy normal. There's something there. Over the years, I've done things using fashion and clothing. Years ago, I remember in the 60s, Eldridge Cleaver, I have to make sure of this ——— came out with a pair of pants. There were a few ads for them in magazines. I remember thinking: 'Oh my god, these pants are crazy'. They were black and white. At one point, someone asked me to do an edition, and I thought, 'Well, let's just make the Eldridge Cleaver pants.' It was a whole thing of trying to find images of the pants! Then there was the thing of trying to get permission from the estate. Of course, they were completely against it. I thought: 'I'll just make them anyway'. I thought the pants were black on one side and white on the other, like a kind of integration, but that wasn't what they were. They had some sort of sock in front, so your dick would go in the sock."

WVB: No!

PMC: "It had a sock sticking out the front, and you would stick your dick in, in the sock, which was made of the same material as the pants. I thought that the pants were black on one side, so the division of the pants went right

WALTER VAN BEIRENDONCK
LET'S TELL A FAIRYTALE
Spring-Summer 1987
Photo: Carel Fonteyne

W.&L.T. – WILD AND LETHAL TRASH
KILLER / ASTRAL TRAVEL / 4D-Hi-D
Spring-Summer 1996
Photo: Ronald Stoops

WALTER VAN BEIRENDONCK
REVOLUTION
Autumn-Winter 2001–2002
Photo: Elisabeth Broekaert

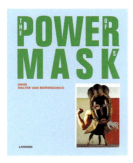

POWERMASK – THE POWER OF MASKS
Exhibition catalogue, Wereldmuseum Rotterdam
1/09/2017–7/01/2018
© Walter Van Beirendonck & Paul Boudens

WALTER VAN BEIRENDONCK
I HAVE SEEN THE FUTURE...
Spring-Summer 2025
Photo: Nick Soland

down the dick ——— half the dick and one leg was black, and half the dick and the other leg was white. So, we made them. They tried to sell them; I think they sold one pair." (laughs)

WVB: Were they commercialised?

PMC: "Yeah, and as soon as I got through making them, I found the image. I realised I had got it completely wrong." (laughs)

WVB: You interpreted it differently.

PMC: "I had sort of made these integrated pants, black on one side, white on the other. And Cleaver had done this thing where they were all white in the front and black in the back; that's how it was. But the dick, the sock, was all black. It was a black dick sock. I got it wrong. I think that I made one pair right. I've done it two or three times where I've made somebody else's thing and completely got it wrong. At that point, I came up with a new piece. My integrated, got-it-wrong Eldridge Cleaver pants, is some sort of collaboration with Eldridge Cleaver." (laughs)

WVB: So, you were like a fashion designer.

PMC: "Yeah, but nobody ever bought my pants. I've really thought about your fashion. When I was a kid, my mother made me a clown suit, quite great. Like the wrong Cleaver pants, it was green on one half and yellow on the other. The split went right up the middle. When she first made it, it had baggy pants and was really big on me. The sleeves hung down. I wore that suit every Halloween for years, I don't know, fuckin' six or seven years. But the suit always fit."

WVB: It was huge.

PMC: "At some point, it fit just below my knees. I kept getting bigger, and the clown suit always stayed the same, but every year it was a new look. It had a dunce hat, a pointed hat, I think it was yellow on one side and green on the other, like a court jester, half and half. It had this collar and then it had big red pom-poms that went down the front and up the hat. When I looked at your work, I often thought of that clown suit. At a certain point, I was going to make it in an edition and people could buy it. It only came in one size. You could pretty much fit anybody. Maybe you could make it in two sizes. It had a story to go with it about Halloween trick-or-treating, where you go from house to house and get candy. We'd go out until 1 o'clock in the morning, going from house to house, and we'd always end up a long way from home. In order to get the suit off, it had a zipper or some buttons down the back. I remember we were with my friends, and we were a mile away from home or something, and I had to pee. I couldn't get the suit off."

WVB: Someone had to help you.

PMC: "I peed in the clown suit. I always thought I should remake the clown suit and people could wear it. But it's not completed until you pee in the clown suit. You have to pee in it."

WVB: That's funny. (laughs)

PMC: "When you've peed in the clown suit, then it's finished. The person who now owns the clown suit has completed the clown suit once they've peed in it."

WVB: In my last collection, the clown was a main inspiration. It wasn't a funny collection. I was telling the story that the world is burning, and I'm still smiling, the world is burning, and I'm still dancing, the world is burning, and I'm still happy. I was using the character of the clown, this personalisation of that happy-sad feeling we all experience today. I was using small, typical clown elements. The smiley face, tiny hats. I also made T-shirts that you can turn around and choose to show the 'happy' or 'sad' side. If you want to wear a happy or sad face, just flip your T-shirt 180 degrees. I have been playing with these characters and elements in fashion as well. How did you get to know my work? Was it when I contacted you or through the exhibition?

PMC: "No, it was actually in a funny way... I've always been a magazine freak. Always. It's always about magazines for me. Pre-social media and pre-iPhone, I would stop at magazine stores and pick up magazines. I was always looking at fashion magazines. And at some point, I knew of you, some of your work. I didn't know that you lived in Belgium. I didn't know any of that. I just knew that in Europe, there's this fashion going on. I didn't know who you were, but I knew the work from images; it stood out. I've always had a kind of interest in fashion. I was good friends with Azzedine Alaïa. That happened through another friend who lived in France. Knowing Azzedine was really just knowing another artist. That's how I looked at it. There's always been an interest, mainly through magazines. And now I'm just addicted to Instagram. Being addicted, I know I have to really be careful. It's the same with magazines."

WVB: It's great that you knew Azzedine Alaïa, he was a really nice person. I met him a few times, I didn't know him very well, but I would say quite well. I saw him from time to time, he visited the school when I was head of the department and he sat on the jury for the graduating class. He told me once: 'What is so amazing about your work is that you can express more through one T-shirt than other people tell through an entire collection'. He was really kind to me in terms of how he viewed my work. It's sad that he's not here anymore.

PMC: "It was really sad and shocking when he died."

WVB: Such a pity. (*sighs*)
Another great memory was when I came to LA and you gave my friends (*Dirk Van Saene, Paul Boudens, Inge Grognard and Ronald Stoops, ed. note*) and me a tour of your studio. Of course, I was really star-struck to see you in person because I was not expecting that you yourself would be guiding us around. You were building the forest back then. Seeing the studio was such a fantastic experience. Walking around in the forest, seeing the different stories, the houses...

PMC: "It's still there. We're moving out of one of them."

WVB: I saw pictures of another studio; I don't think it was the same.

PMC: "We're getting out of one of them and consolidating everything. We don't need as much space right now. A lot of the studio right now is storage. I'm still making sculptures, but not nearly the same way I did before. A lot of it is about performance video and editing."

WVB: You must really enjoy making films and movies. When I saw 'CSSC – It Begins The Coach The Skull', it featured a Louis Vuitton handbag. I found it surreal to suddenly see that popping up in the context of your video performance. Was it ironic?

PMC: "It's about these six people in a stagecoach travelling through the West. They're dressed in an 1800s period way, to a degree. And the stagecoach is an authentic stagecoach with real horses. But on the other side of that, the names of the characters were anachronistic. I played Ronald Reagan, and my wife in the video was Nancy Reagan. There was a character in the coach named Jesus Christ, and then you had Mary Magdalene, and Adam and Eve. You knew my name was Ronald Reagan, and my wife was Nancy Reagan, but I had a beard, so I didn't look like Ronald Reagan. The two innocent characters were Adam who was a dentist and Eve, an actress living in Silver Lake that did commercials. So: what is this? It's not a period piece. Jesus Christ wore a pink suit. There's this element of mixing. It's about the mushing together of America.

The inside of that coach was like America. Adam and Eve didn't know each other, but they represented the young innocents, and Jesus Christ, Mary Magdalene, Ronald and Nancy were libertines. Nancy and Ronald know each other, but Jesus Christ and Mary Magdalene don't know each other; and you're not sure if they're using their real names. But what you do realise quickly is that these older characters, Ronald, Nancy, Jesus and Mary, as libertines, know that there's a game to be played. The game is the abuse of the two innocent characters Adam and Eve. It's really about power, libertines and abuse. Adam the dentist clutches the Louis Vuitton bag, that's where he keeps his dental equipment. It was actually a Louis Vuitton Murakami bag. At one point, Jesus Christ takes the bag away from Adam and throws it out of the window. He throws the Louis Vuitton bag out of the moving stagecoach. The artists engaging with the fashion world. There's an idea in there. It's like a kind of shock. The Louis Vuitton Murakami bag tells you that despite the costumes, this isn't happening in the 1800s."

WVB: Are you travelling to Europe soon, or do you have any plans to?

PMC: "I was in Belgium for my show at Xavier Hufkens in 2023 and then at Max Hetzler in Berlin. I'm going to do a show in London in January 2025. I might come to Europe in the fall, but I don't know what will happen. I'm not travelling as much."

WVB: I would definitely like to see you when you're in Europe and bring you some beer. Because you like Delirium Tremens so much, the beer with the pink elephants. Is that something you discovered in Belgium?

PMC: "A long time ago, I was in a bar in Belgium looking up at a big blackboard, and it was just the names of beers. Just rows and rows. I thought, when I looked up there, it was the menu for food. I had never seen such a thing."

WVB: They were all different beers. (*laughs*)

PMC: "I remember, around that time, seeing the beer bottle for Delirium and thinking the name was great. I had made pieces called 'Delirium', so there was an association with that name. There came this point where I began to drink Delirium beer, and that was it. People started to notice. I would get bottles of Delirium beer and Delirium T shirts. A while back, someone gave me a box of Delirium Tremens umbrellas. It became a story where 'Paul only drinks Delirium'. But that wasn't true. A friend, Elyse Poppers, who played White Snow, brought

PAUL McCARTHY
Pinocchio Pipenose Householddilemma, 1994
Performance, video, installation, photographs

© Paul McCarthy. Courtesy the artist and Hauser & Wirth.

ELDRIDGE CLEAVER
Advertisement, 1975
Found image

PAUL McCARTHY
Memory Mistake of the Eldridge Cleaver Pants, 2008
Corduroy, zipper, snaps, thread, mannequin, stand
124.5 × 44.5 × 35.6 cm

© Paul McCarthy. Courtesy the artist and Hauser & Wirth.

PAUL McCARTHY
CSSC Coach Stage Stage Coach, 2017
Performance, video, installation, photographic series
Directed by Paul McCarthy and Damon McCarthy

© Paul McCarthy. Courtesy the artist and Hauser & Wirth.
Photo: Edmund Barr

PAUL McCARTHY
CSSC Coach Stage Stage Coach, Way Station, 2017
Performance, video, installation, photographic series
Directed by Paul McCarthy and Damon McCarthy

© Paul McCarthy. Courtesy the artist and Hauser & Wirth.
Photo: Ryan Chin, Edmund Barr, Damon McCarthy

PAUL McCARTHY
CSSC Coach Stage Stage Coach, Dogs Attack, 2017
Performance, video, installation, photographic series
Directed by Paul McCarthy and Damon McCarthy

© Paul McCarthy. Courtesy the artist and Hauser & Wirth.
Photo: Ryan Chin

PAUL McCARTHY
Tree (Inflatable), 2014
Green vinyl, fans
2438.4 × 1371.6 × 1371.6 cm

© Paul McCarthy. Courtesy the artist and Hauser & Wirth.
Photo: Marc Domage

me St. Bernardus beer years ago when we first started working together, so I drink that too. It's another Belgian beer. I have to be able to connect with them beyond just the taste."

WVB: Is it Belgian? I don't know St. Bernardus beer.

PMC: "It was a bit of a joke. Before craft beers became popular, you couldn't get them in LA. It became about getting this beer and drinking this beer like a joke, it's been a joke, right?"

WVB: It's also because of the packaging with the pink elephant is beautiful.

PMC: "Right, and the white bottle. By the side of our house, there's a pile of Belgian beer bottles."

(*Both laugh*)

PMC: "There was a period when I was saving Belgian beer bottles and corks. I was saving the corks. It was crazy, so now I have boxes of corks of Belgian beer. I have always been really interested in the artists of Belgium. There was something about Belgium. Marcel Broodthaers. It goes way back for me. I first discovered him in an issue of *Avalanche* magazine. *Avalanche* was a performance and conceptual art magazine, one of the best art magazines of the 70s... Of all time. But there was an image in the magazine. I don't think it said anything. It didn't have his name on it. It was just a full page of Marcel Broodthaers standing next to a very small piano. There was a catalogue inventory number on the piano. It was strange, him in this pinstripe suit next to the small piano. Very strange. I was obsessed with the image. When my daughter was born, after about a year or so, I went and bought a small piano. We still have it. And the Magritte Vache paintings, like the one of the man with multiple smoking pipes. I think of these Vache paintings and Marcel Broodthaers work as significant."

WVB: There are a lot of contemporary artists doing well in Belgium.

PMC: "I like the temperament of Belgium, how I imagine it."

WVB: Do you know Ensor? It's 'Ensor year' now, celebrating his work in all different fields. The MoMu Fashion Museum in Antwerp is having an exhibition about make-up and masks inspired by or as a homage to Ensor. It's incredible work.
There's something totally different I wanted to discuss. I was totally shocked when you put up the blow-up green 'Tree' installation at Place Vendôme in Paris, and it had to be taken down because people were attacking it with knives. I thought that reaction to your work was so shocking. What did you think of that? Were you upset or surprised?

PMC: "I didn't quite expect it, I guess. I hadn't thought about what it was. I didn't really understand. I knew something about the history of that plaza, but, I didn't understand what it meant at that moment. I didn't know demonstrations had happened. I wasn't really aware."

WVB: Of the sensitivity surrounding that place?

PMC: "For a certain part of the population. It was a lot about French pride, French nationalism and conservatism. Yes, sure, you're putting a butt plug in the middle of Paris."

WVB: How strong the statement was.

PMC: "I had put inflatable butt plugs in parks before, or a big inflatable pile of shit. At the time I did the green tree plug I was doing this big piece the 'Chocolate Factory' at La Monnaie de Paris."

WVB: It's so weird that that butt plug was causing such a violent reaction. In Rotterdam as well, the moving of the gnome with the butt plug... It's weird that a simple thing that has a connotation to sex becomes the enemy of so many people. They see it as 'danger, danger, we can't allow this'.

PMC: "I think America is pretty volatile in that way, take what happened the other day." (*The assassination attempt on Donald Trump, ed. note*).

WVB: Europe is terrible at the moment, the surge of the extreme right. It's strange how politics are going in the wrong direction. It's such a shame.

PMC: "There are parts of my work where there's censorship going on, within the art world too."

WVB: Can you really feel that censorship?

PMC: "Oh, yes. I'll be asked to do a layout for an art magazine, and when it's finished, they'll say: 'We can't print this'. That has been ongoing. There's a kind of censorship where they refuse to show something and won't talk about it; they just don't show it. At times, I've self-censored. 'Woah, maybe I can't put that out right now. It'll be misunderstood.' There's this thing of literal interpretation. Not seeing the work as caricature, satire or metaphor but as literal. You play the character of Adolf Hitler, and they take it literally. Language, right? It's this thing of conservatism within the art world, a form of Stalinism. To want things to be literal. How do you talk about Walt Disney without using Walt Disney or Mickey Mouse? How do you talk about fascism without engaging the subject? It removes a lot of the emotion; it removes the feeling. Literal is just didactic talk. There's a conservatism around the subject of art that really affects what art is or can be. You realise that kind of work is not for everybody. It's not for everybody because they can't go there. Some people can't look at an expression and dissect it or understand what's being said. They can only deal with what's on the surface. Sometimes, you just kind of know that there's no way this is going to be understood."

WVB: We are forced to think twice now before we do something. I remember how spontaneous I used to be in my drawings and sketches. But now you're forced to think: 'Can I do this? Can I reference this kind of inspiration?' It's a completely different time.

PMC: "I don't think I censor myself in making work. But showing it lately has been different. I pretty much show all of it, but I have said a couple of times: 'I can't show that there'. Or I have asked myself: 'Is it worthwhile? Is there a reason to do it?' Making the work is a lot about showing the work, but there's an entire body of work right now that I am still determining when to show. There's no opportunity to do it. Nobody will show it."

WVB: There's no opportunity because certain museums or galleries aren't willing to show things that they think are too difficult or risky for them.

PMC: "They're concerned about their money, there's that side to it too. Funding and institutions. Money and funding affects what gets seen. The work I have been doing in the last few years, most of it hasn't been seen for a number of reasons, not enough money, can't finish parts of it, no place to show it, too controversial. But it still goes on as if one day it will be finished and seen."

WVB: Limited possibilities are sometimes better than having too many.

PMC: "Money and making fabricated work doesn't always create the best work. I have made a lot of pieces that I've personally rejected because they're very much about money. They were good experiments for me to have made, I had to make them at the time. They seemed right at the time, but looking back... A number of those pieces just have to do with the money that was available. A lot of the pieces that mean the most to me were the pieces that were done without money. Of course there are pieces that money made happen that are very important to me. Like a door opened up and something came out."

WVB: I once made a collection named *REVOLUTION*. I made it at a time when I was running out of money, had no possibilities but still wanted to continue. I just bought a bunch of fabrics, mainly fabrics for furniture and curtains, 60s and 70s stuff. I made a whole collection inspired by 'Les Incroyables' in rather extreme shapes and forms. It's one of the collections I'm most known for. They have looks from that collection at LACMA in LA. They have it in New York. It was a small collection, just 15 looks. I couldn't produce any more. I didn't even commercialise it. Just purely made it for continuity. It's one of my most important ones.

PMC: "I think that's true."

WVB: There's a close tie between fashion and art, one way or another. It was fantastic to talk to you, so nice to get to know you a little bit better. If you're in Europe, I'd love to meet up or see you.

PMC: "Next year, I'll go to Europe more. In 2025."

WVB: That's good. I'll send you the books when they're finished, and Dominique will work with you on the final text.

DNZ: I'll send it to Dylan. This was an amazing conversation. This is also a TV show I would watch. And I really hope the clown suit that isn't finished until you pee in it comes out soon.

WVB: Nice stories, right?

DNZ: Amazing stories. Thank you so much, Paul.

WVB: Thank you, Paul! I hope to see you soon, and we'll stay in touch. Dylan, thank you very much for helping to make this happen. Bye, everyone!

PMC: "Okay, cool. Bye!"

(To be continued!)

HARDCORE WALTER SINCE 1985

BE
BOLD
BE
BRAVE

THE BEST WAY TO PREDICT THE FUTURE IS TO CREATE IT

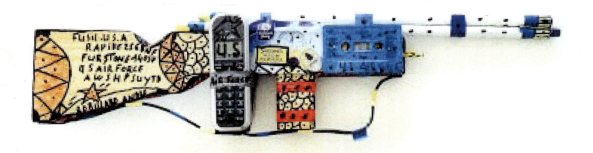

CHERISH CREATIVITY

P

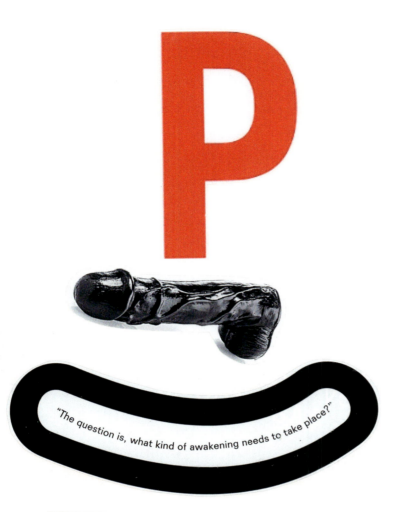

"The question is, what kind of awakening needs to take place?"

FULL FRONTAL

apocalypse always sells.

Glorification of any principle

BAN
BANALITY

ALL YOU NEED IS FAITH & TRUST

AND A LITTLE BIT OF STARDUST

AND A LITTLE BIT OF STARDUST

ALL YOU NEED IS FAITH & TRUS

Junko Shimada

WAITING FOR WAR

Ted Owens
How to Contact Space People (1969)
Mensa member Ted Owens (1920–1987) claimed to have conversations with Space Intelligences (SIs), energy beings sometimes appearing in the guise of insects. He explained that repeated head injuries he'd suffered earlier in life were caused by the SIs so that he could later communicate with them. He explains how to get in touch with them yourself in *How to Contact Space People*. Calling himself "Dr PK", he later claimed to be able to control the weather and earthquakes, predict saucer landings and bend metal objects.

BE BOLD BE BRAVE BE BOLD BE BRAVE BE BOLD BE
BE BRAVE BE BOLD BE BRAVE BE BOLD BE BRAVE BE
BE BOL
BE BRA
BE BOL
BE BRA
BE BOL
BE BRA
BE BOL
BE BRA
BE BOL
BE BRA
BE BOL
BE BRA
BE BOL
BE BRA
BE BOL
BE BRA
BE BOL
BE BRA
BE BOL
BE BRA
BE BOL
BE BRA
BE BOL
BE BRA
BE BOL
BE BRA
BE BOL
BE BRA
BE BOL

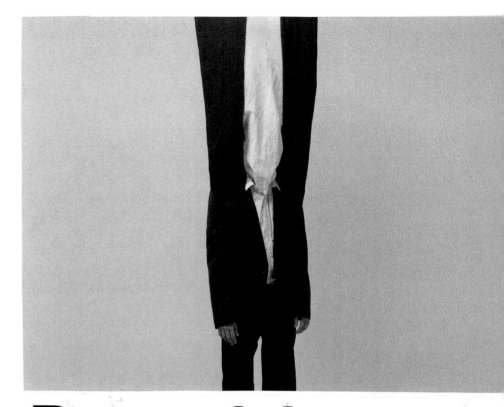

Powerful Structure Nr.1:

SUPERSUPER!

THE BEAUTY AND THE DARK

BE BRAVE BE BOLD BE BRAVE BE BOLD BE BRAVE BE
BE BOLD BE BRAVE BE BOLD BE BRAVE BE BOLD BE

BELIEVE

magic

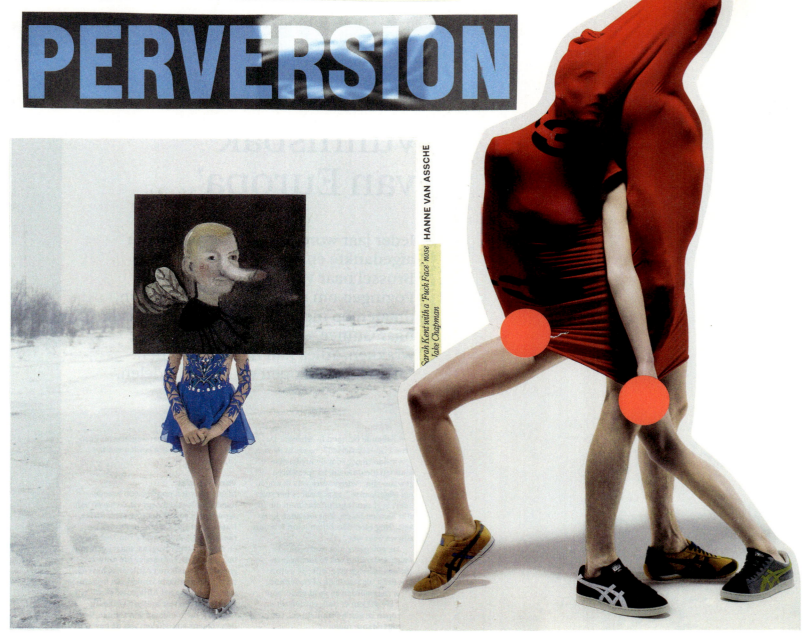

AWAKEN A NEW WORLD NOW

"'Hey, asswipe, I'm a cock-suckin' movie star, so you can just lick my dirty brown ass!'"

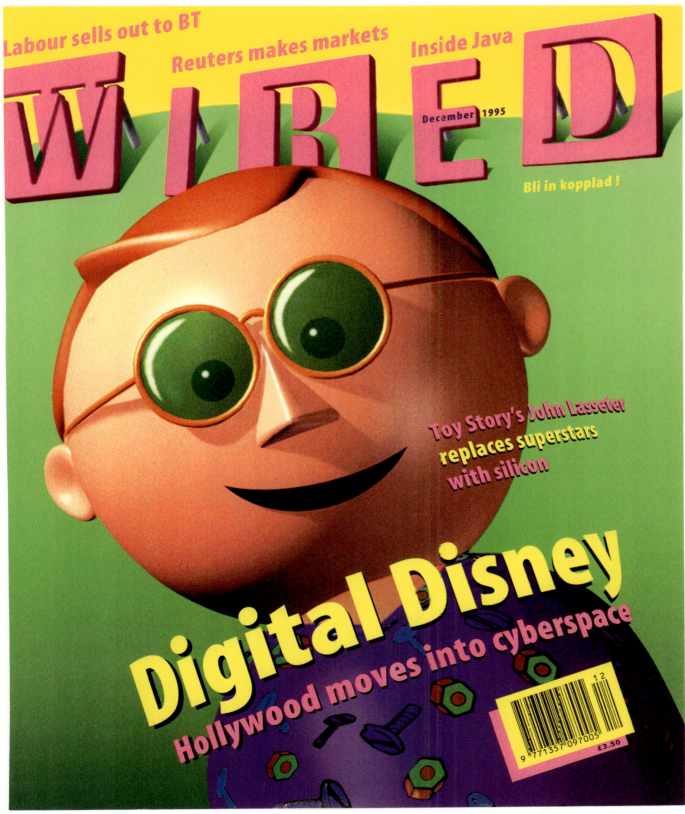

step between different worlds

Subscribe!

incarnation of a hindu deity

life is the ultimate technology.

Let There Be Technosphere

If you've ever dreamed of building a new world on the digital frontier, then perhaps Technosphere is for you. Here you can build not just the world, but also the creatures that inhabit it. Frankensteins-by-the-numbers can be created from the creature-kit parts available at *http://lcp20.lond-inst.ac.uk/technosphere/index.html*. The more ambitious can build baby from scratch with a 3-D modelling package. Turn junior loose and then watch as it evolves, mutates, forages for food or, maybe, gets tragically blown away by the digital whirlwinds that traverse Technosphere's fractal landscape.

Technosphere is a collaboration between several artists and computer animators: Jane Prophet, Gordon Selley, Andrew Kind, and Julian Saunderson. They see it as a new form of artwork that erases the barrier between spectator and participant. They hope to create a string of virtual worlds, linked together into a kind of Technoverse. And on the seventh day they will apply to renew their Arts Council funding. Technosphere: *technosphere@cairn.demon.co.uk* – Hari Kunzru

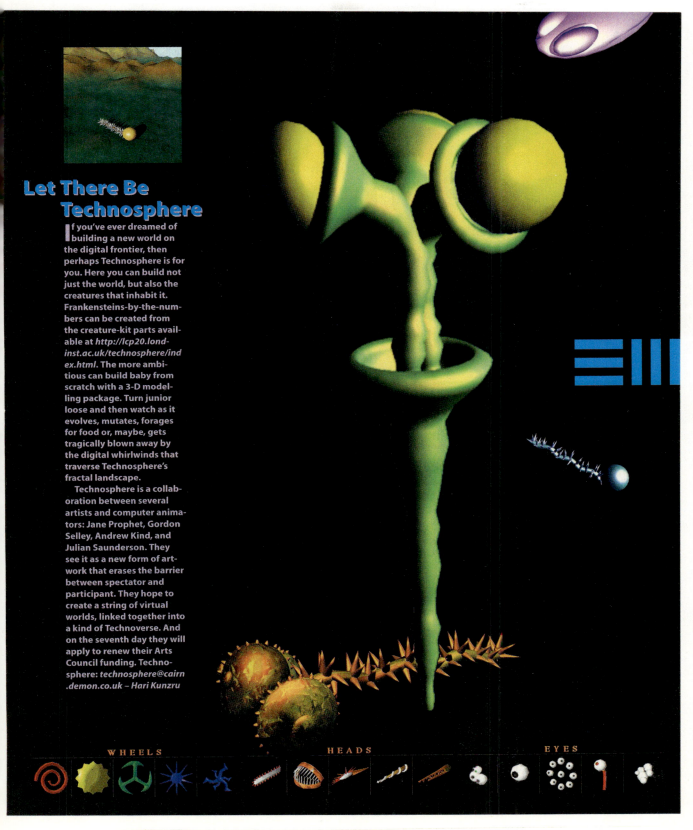

an electronic embodiment in cyberspace

DEMAND FREEDOM!

from screen to life

avatars the fashionstatement of the 21st century

CONTENTS? TESTING.

dream machines
The Ultimate Dashboard

MARRAKESCH, 1993

MAROKKANISCHER FETISCH AUS EINGEWICKELTEN VOGELFEDERN

avatar locomotion

NEW TYPE THAT MAKES A STATEMENT

HOW MUCH IS THAT WORLD IN THE WINDOW?

tailor your appearance

UNDERCOVER
A LONE WOLF BY INCLINATION AS WELL AS BY DESIGN, THE PRIVATE DETECTIVE LIVES ON HIS WITS. QUIETLY CONFIDENT, SELF~ASSURED, SOPHISTICATED, ALWAYS GETS A RESULT... AND THAT'S JUST HIS WARDROBE

espionage

FEVER!

classic plastic

SUCK ON THIS

FUTURE

carnal sensations

strange

modern shamans.

voyeuristic gaze

second skin

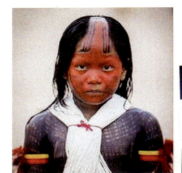
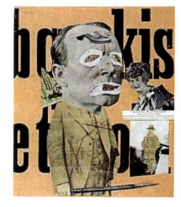

Modern *ultimately eccentric* look.

purity

wild

bodies

domination

Art is not what you see,
Edgar Degas, Franse schilder en beeldhouwer (1834-1917)

heroes

but what you make others see

stick up

REBELLING TO INVENT NEW WORLDS

Freakshow aesthetics

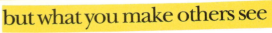

s t a r

SMILE

TECHNO

virtual virtuoso

FUTURE BEAUTY

BLOWING UP HARDCORE

lust

uncontrollable

A *subversive exterior*

Magical Thinking

Mashups

cut out for an

neoclassical

eroticism

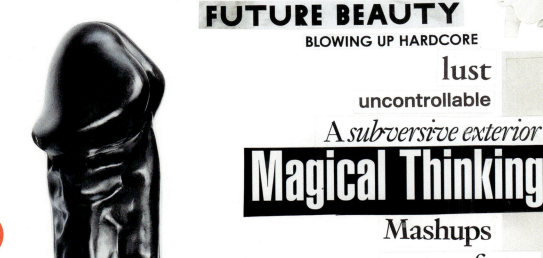

wizard

think punk

evoked
romantic

dress to thrill

and pigs can fly

8 VIRTUES
HONESTY-telling the truth-BLUE
COMPASSION-showing love-YELLOW
VALOR-not running away from situations-RED
JUSTICE-being equal-GREEN
SACRIFICE-giving yourself-ORANGE
HONOR-upholding your duty-PURPLE
SPIRITUALITY-enlightenment-WHITE
HUMILITY-treat everyone as equals-BLACK

just plug in!

Does this sound like fun

It can be.

UNBRIDLED SEX IN BARS AND BACKROOMS

Mighty Morphine Power Rangers

MUD & MOO

In queste immagini gli Art Club 2000 durante alcune performance.

**fake I.D.
UNDERCOVER
BEHIND THE MASK**

STOP
VIOLENCE

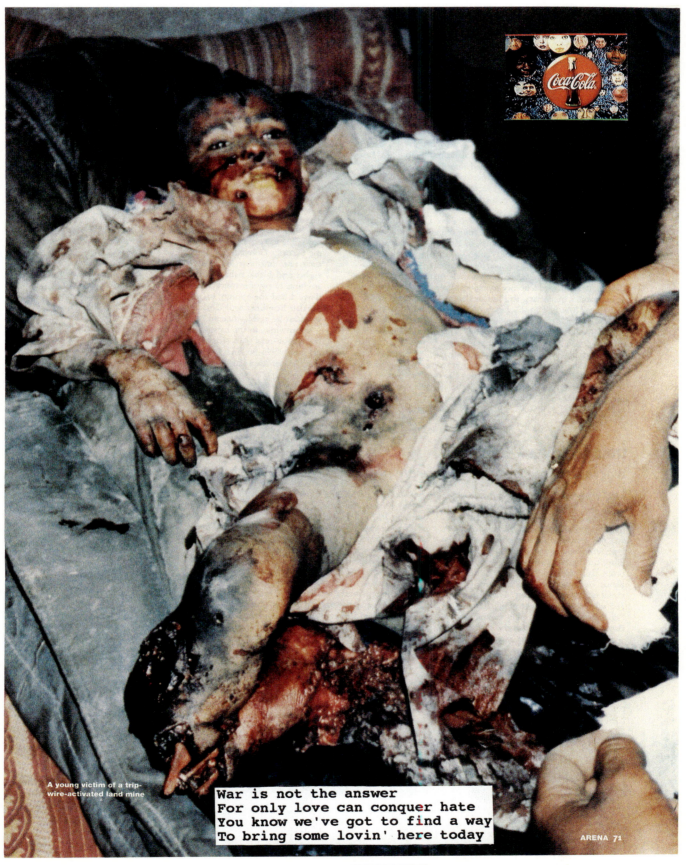

NOT JUST A PRETTY FACE
KATHRYN BIGELOW REFLECTS ON

feeling supersonic

Buy off-the-shelf avatars

DEFEND LOVE

CONTROL?

Never go into the jungle,
unless you're ready to go all the way.

— *Apocalypse Now*

Faster, Gravity! Kill! Kill!

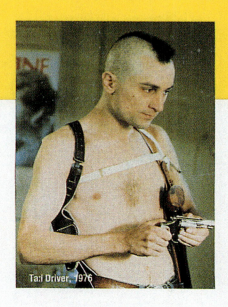

DELUSION

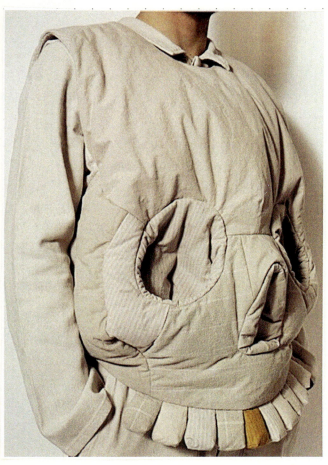
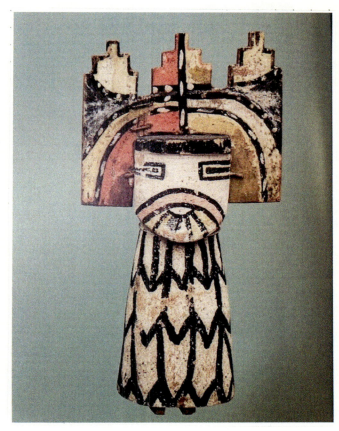

GLOWALTERADIATE

Yes I'm Gonna Be A Star

Daring Devilish Darling UZI

BE SURE BE SAFE

ORGASM

Colorful New World

THIS body IS NOT TO BE WATCHED. IT IS TO BE EXPERIENCED.

CATCH A FALLING STAR...

...GUARDIAN ANGELS...

See for yourself!
All you want in your dream
W. & L.T. IS HERE!

WILD AND LETHAL TRASH !

W. & L.T.
mania

A new and deadly force in the playground is this life-size replica of the militiaman's little helper, the UZI machine pistol. Matt black and recoilless, just like the real thing, this battery-powered machine *water* pistol fires 250 squirts per minute with a range of 30 feet. The UZI has been one of the more popular adult toys in recent US action movies and featured earlier this year in a FACE documentary (yep, *that* one). In his last death-dealing comic book *Cobra*, along with Loden overcoat and Ray-Ban Aviators, Stallone wore one to maximum effect. The sinister Laramie toy corporation, who manufacture the water-powered version, had a sales bonanza. At £8.99 from Hamley's, Regent St, London W1, it's just the thing to offset that PFLP camouflage jacket. For violence loving boys and girls everywhere.

WE WISH YOU PEACE

*Animal experimentation:
the debate continues*

WHITE TRASH

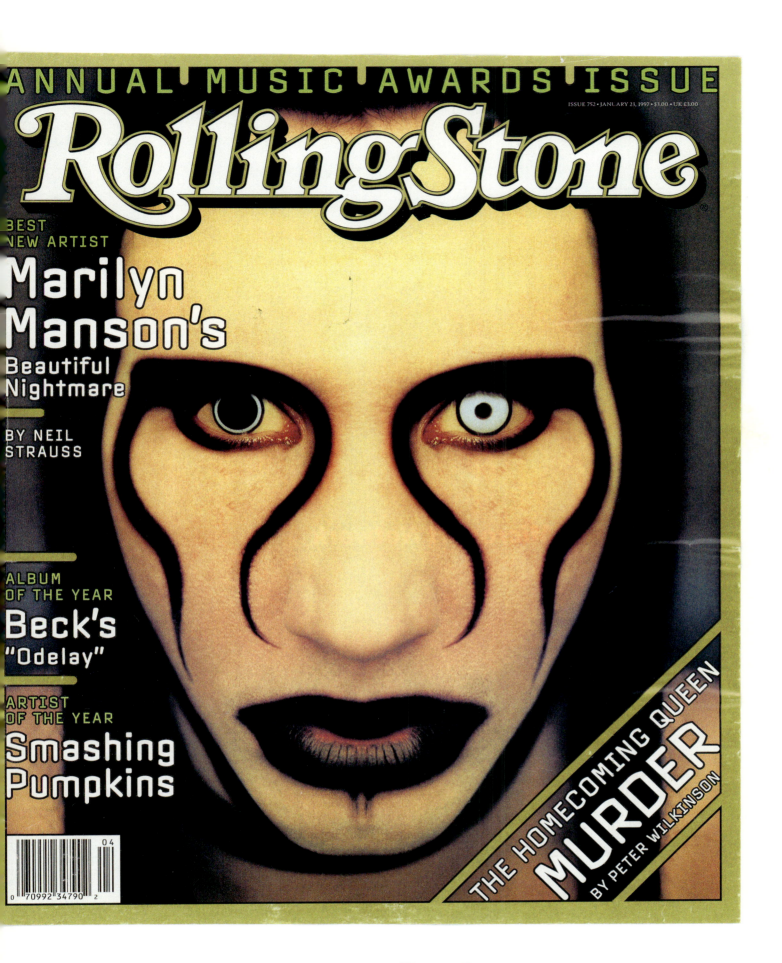

BLACK BEAUTY

FASHION IS DEAD!

HARDCORE HARDCORE HARDCORE HARDCORE HAR
HARDCORE HARDCORE HARDCORE HARDCORE HAR
HARDCORE HARDCORE HARDCORE HARDCORE HAR
HARDCORE HARDCORE HARDCORE HARDCORE HAR
HARDCORE HARDCORE HARDCORE HARDCORE HAR
HARDCORE HARDCORE HARDCORE HARDCORE HAR
HARDCORE HARDCORE
HARDCORE HARDCORE
HARDCORE HARDCORE
HARDCORE HARDCORE
HARDCORE HARDCORE
HARDCORE HARDCORE HERO OFF ALL TIME
HARDCORE HARDCORE
HARDCORE HARDCORE
HARDCORE HARDCORE
HARDCORE HARDCORE
HARDCORE HARDCORE
HARDCORE HARDCORE
HARDCORE HARDCORE
HARDCORE HARDCORE
HARDCORE HARDCORE
HARDCORE HARDCORE
HARDCORE HARDCORE
HARDCORE HARDCORE
HARDCORE HARDCORE HARDCORE HARDCORE HAR
HARDCORE HARDCORE HARDCORE HARDCORE HAR
HARDCORE HARDCORE HARDCORE HARDCORE HAR
HARDCORE HARDCORE HARDCORE HARDCORE HAR
HARDCORE HARDCORE HARDCORE HARDCORE HAR

HARDCORE HARDCORE HARDCORE HARDCORE
HARDCORE HARDCORE HARDCORE HARDCORE
HARDCORE HARDCORE HARDCORE HARDCORE
HARDCORE HARDCORE HARDCORE HARDCORE
HARDCORE HARDCORE HARDCORE HARDCORE
HARDCORE HARDCORE HARDCORE HARDCORE

SURVIVAL OF THE FITTEST: Is this the real world or is it just fantasy? *Planet Of The Apes* unmasked. FILM, page 179

HARDCORE HARDCORE HARDCORE HARDCORE
HARDCORE HARDCORE HARDCORE HARDCORE
HARDCORE HARDCORE HARDCORE HARDCORE
HARDCORE HARDCORE HARDCORE HARDCORE
HARDCORE HARDCORE HARDCORE HARDCORE

DEMAND BEAUTY

Reset
Clinical Cosmology

dimension S

"The old world is dying, and the new world struggles to be born: now is the time of monsters."[1]

WHISPERS:

the crossbreeding of

enigmatic   sibylline   monstrous,

reflection of the

"tip of the tongue"

Gloomy

Fucked-up Objects

SICK OF EASY FASHION

hug

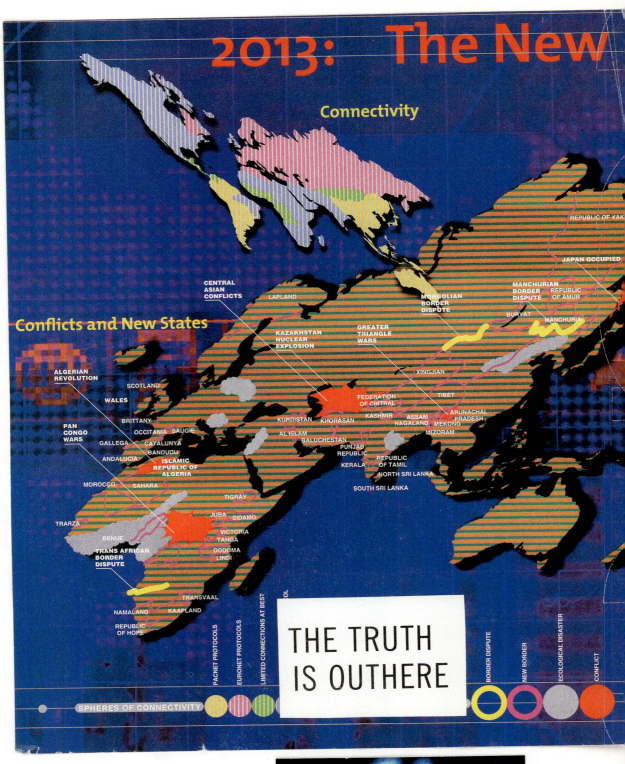

MY PLANET
MY FREEDOM

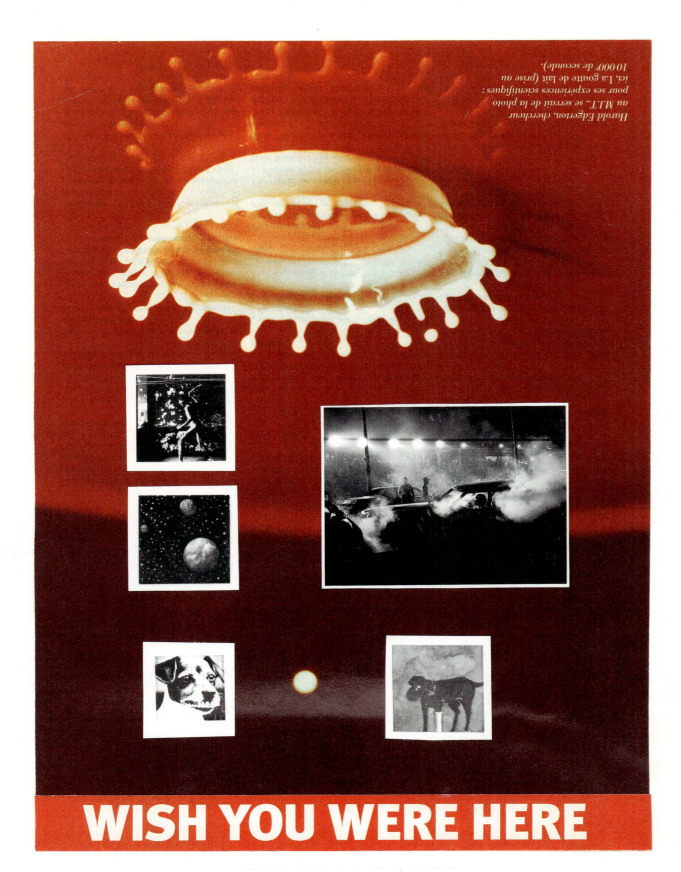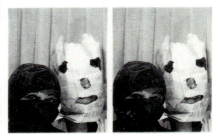

"I'm not saying I have the Perfect Brand but it's probably the Truest shit you've seeN all year."

MENSCHEN '95

KISS ME QUICK

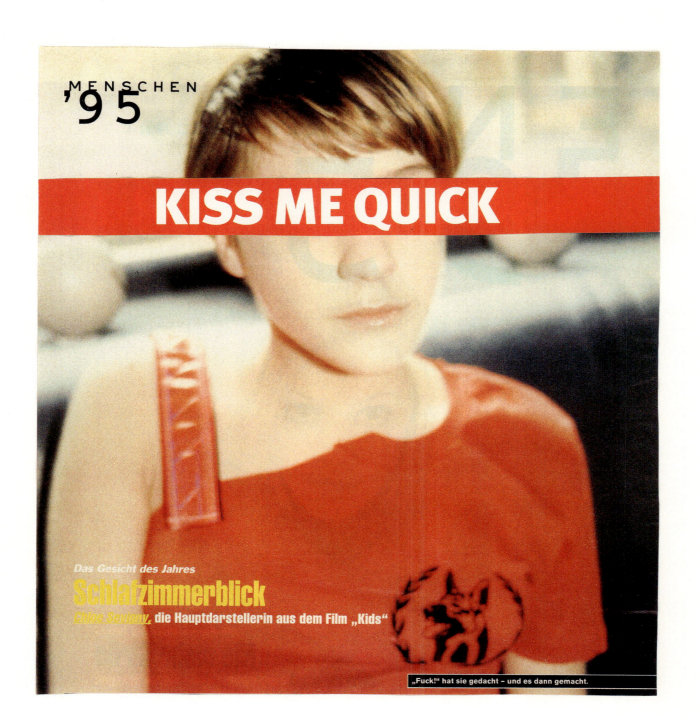

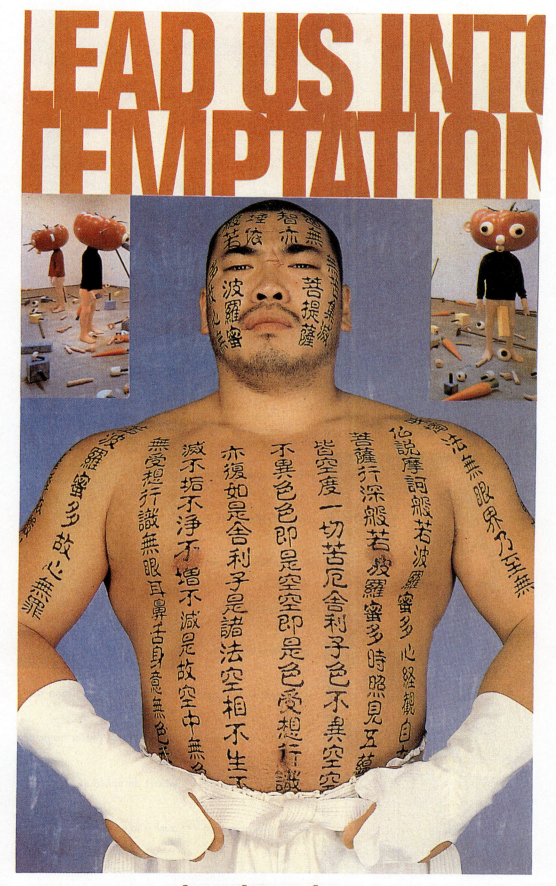

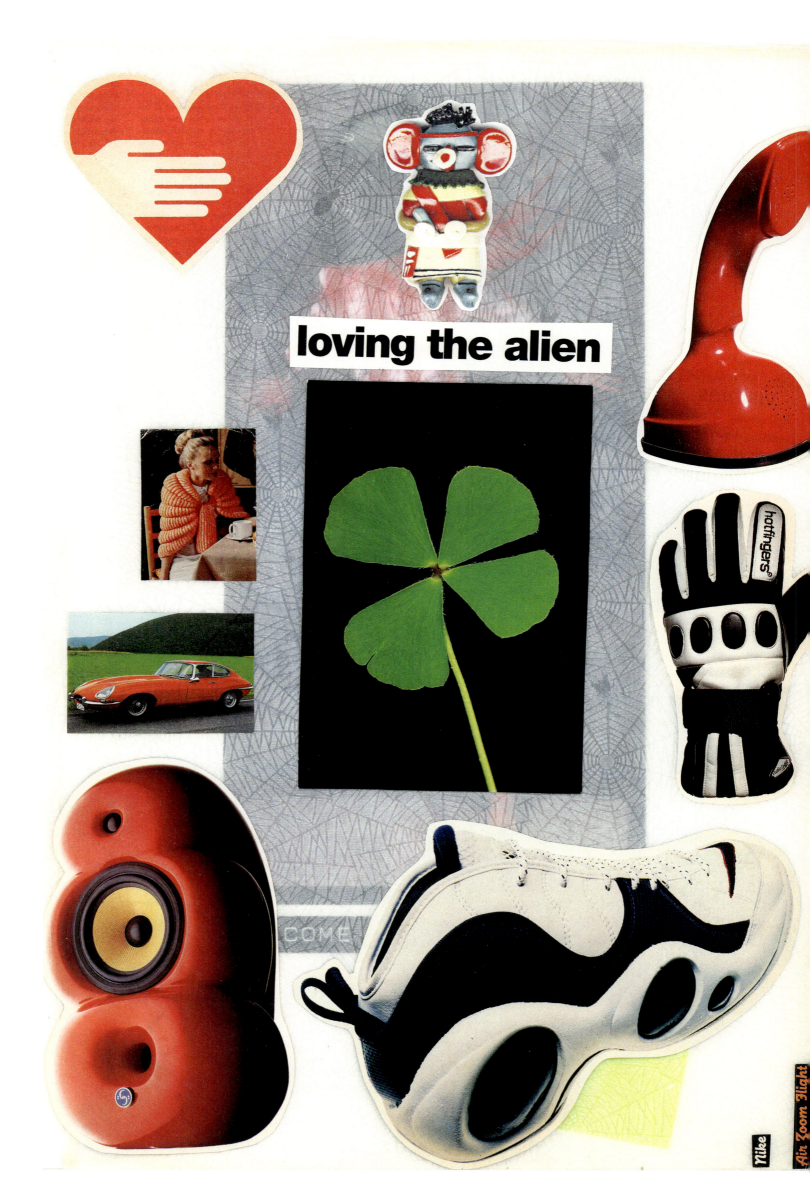

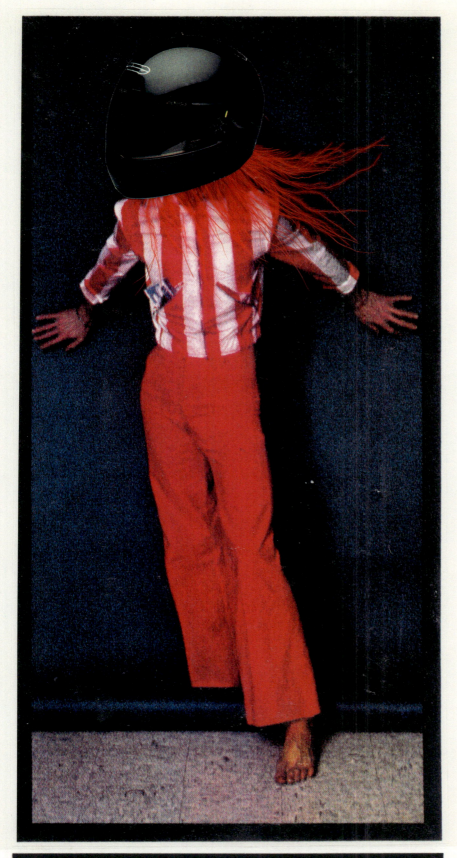

WELCOME LITTLE STRANGER

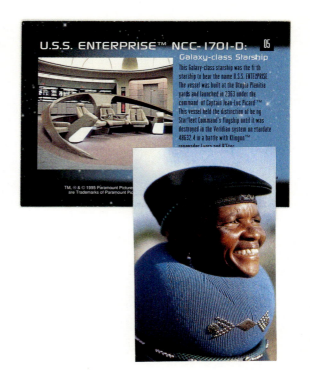

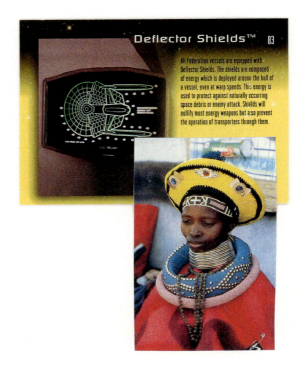

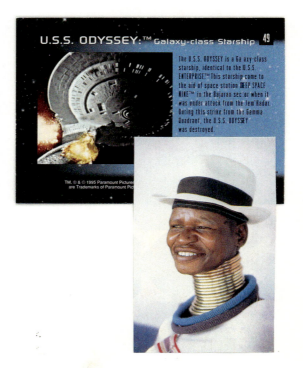

FUTURE BEAUTY

ALIENATE

WELCOME STRANGERS

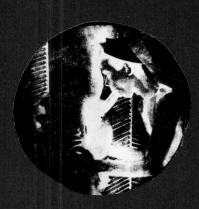

The Ominous Men in Black

I want to build a clock that ticks once a year.

YOU LOOK LIKE A TELEVISION SITTING ON A REFRIGERATOR

love

waving goodbye to a holiday romance

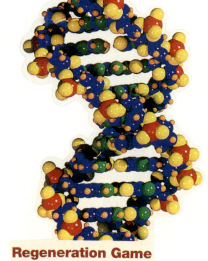

Regeneration Game

WE CAN BE HEROES

art

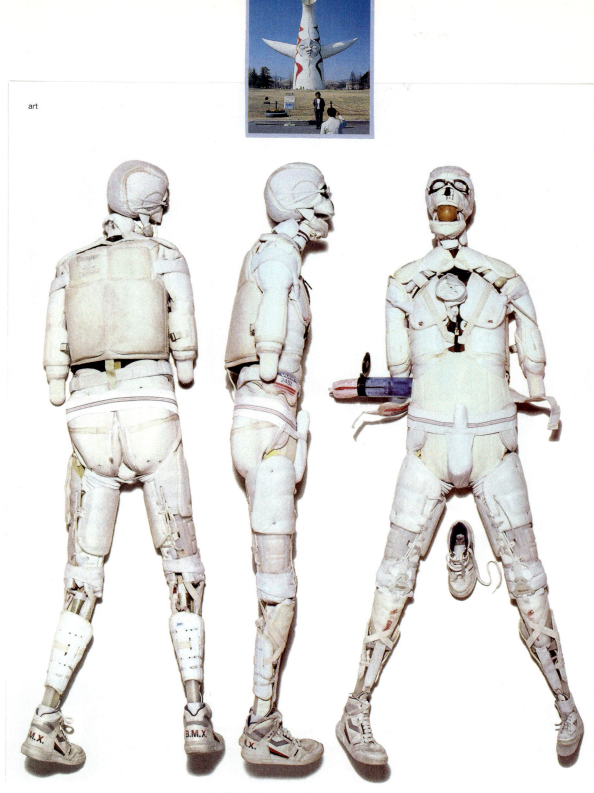

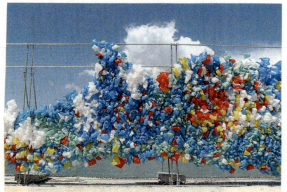

WELCOME LITTLE STRANGER WELCOME LITTLE STR
STRANGER WELCOME LITTLE STRANGER WELCO
WELC
STRAI
WELC
STRAI
WELC
STRAI
WELC
STRAI
WELC
STRAI
WELC
STRAI
WELC
STRAI
WELC
STRAI
WELC
STRAI
WELC
STRAI
WELC
STRAI
WELC
STRAI
WELC
STRANGER WELCOME LITTLE STRANGER WELCO
WELCOME LITTLE STRANGER WELCOME LITTLE STR

Valérie Belin, «Sans titre», 2000. Photographie noir et blanc.

<< BELA BORSODI

PROVOCATIVE
Uncut!

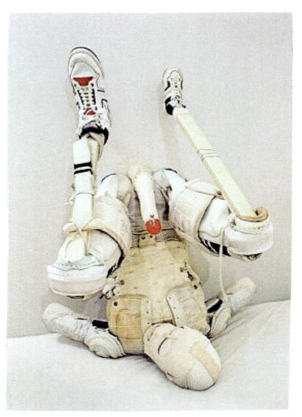

FASHION IS NOT DEAD!

INITIATION

WHOSE LAND IS IT ANYWAY

;-S

FUTURE CAN WINK

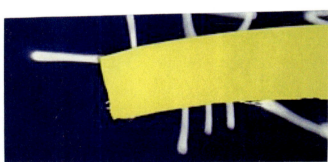
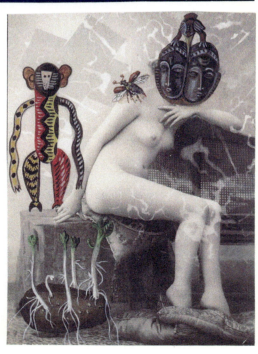

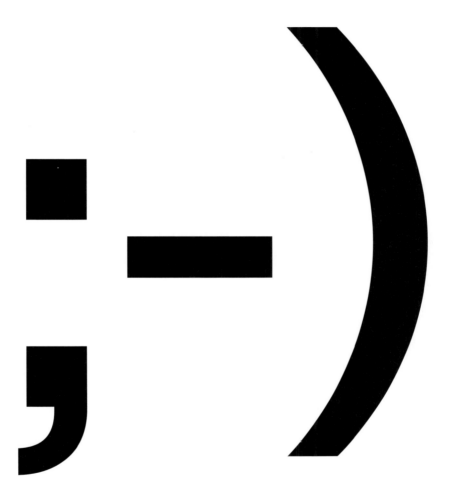

GROW YOUR FUR

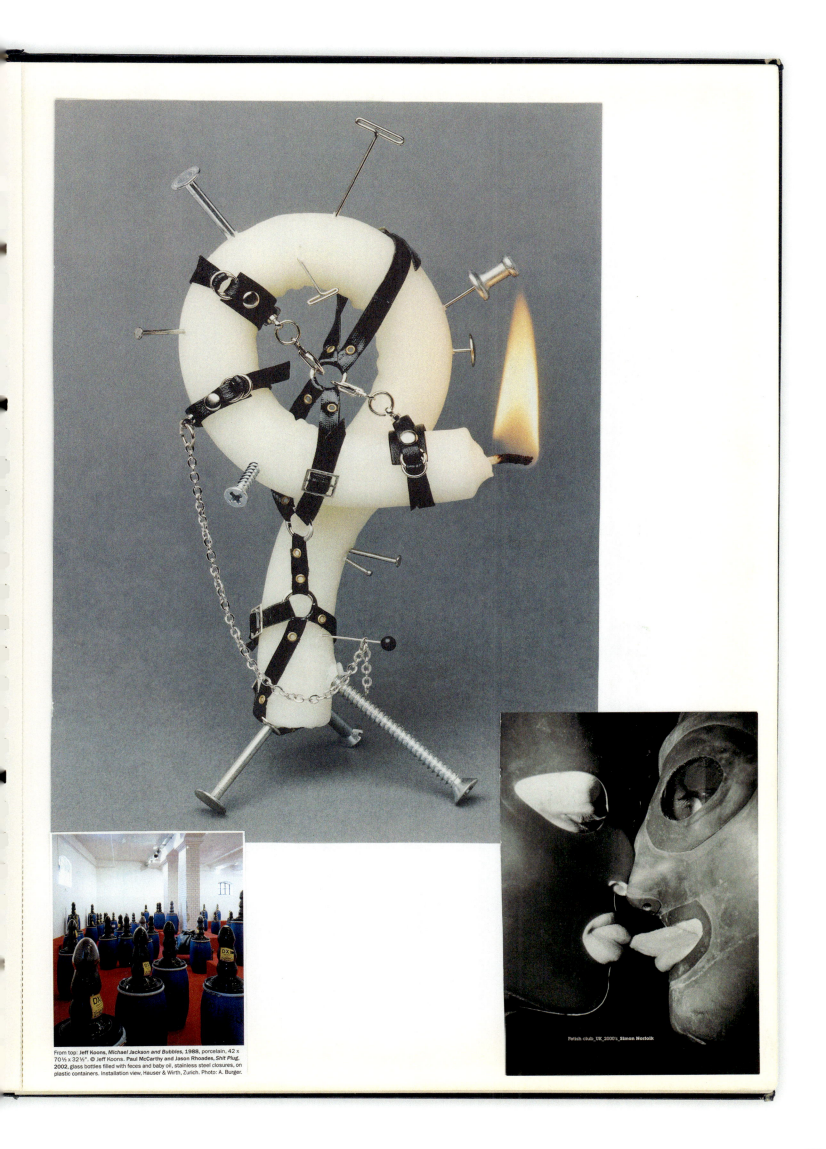

From top: Jeff Koons, *Michael Jackson and Bubbles*, 1988, porcelain, 42 x 70½ x 32½". © Jeff Koons. Paul McCarthy and Jason Rhoades, *Shit Plug*, 2002, glass bottles filled with feces and baby oil, stainless steel closures, on plastic containers. Installation view, Hauser & Wirth, Zurich. Photo: A. Burger.

By learning from history we can avoid future disaster

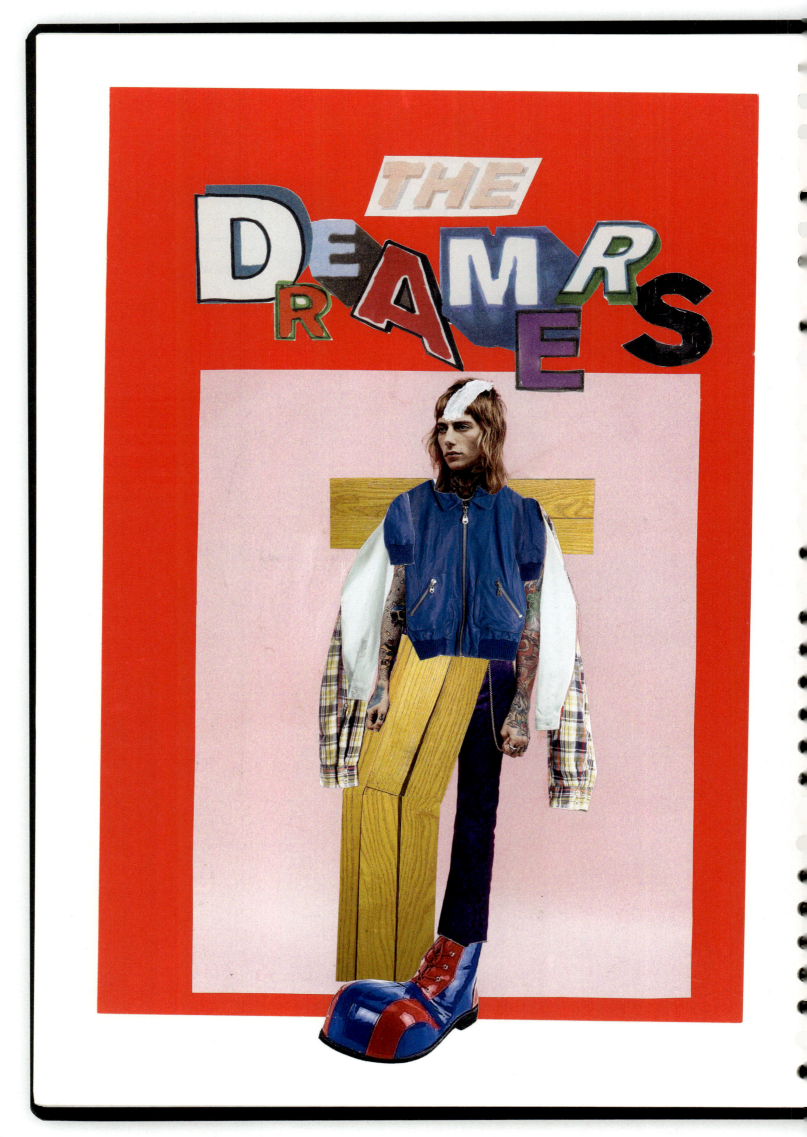

PLEASURE BOYS PLEASURE BOYS PLEASURE BOYS
BOYS PLEASURE BOYS PLEASURE BOYS PLEASURE

Heaven loves ya
The clouds part for ya
Nothing stands in your way
When you're a boy

Clothes always fit ya
Life is a pop of the cherry
When you're a boy

When you're a boy
You can wear a uniform
When you're a boy
Other boys check you out
You get a girl
These are your favourite things
When you're a boy

Boys
Boys
Boys keep swinging
Boys always work it out

PLEASURE BOYS PLEASURE BOYS PLEASURE
BOYS PLEASURE BOYS PLEASURE BOYS PLEASURE

The Source of Pleasure

SLOGANS REMIND YOU OF THE STEPS YOU NEED TO TAKE

SELF PORTRAIT

FEAR OF BEING WEIRD

WEIRD

LIANA FINCK

NO

nement op dat blad leerde kennen via Instagram, doet het anders: zij beeldt zichzelf af aan de hand van een soort venndiagram. Haar gevoel raar te zijn staat centraal, maar de angst om raar te zijn is nog groter. Heel simpel, maar treffend, toont ze hoe allesbepalend dat gevoel kan zijn.'

'Het is een toestand die ik maar al te goed herken. Ik had het als kind al en eigenlijk nog steeds. Je raar voelen, anders dan anderen, maar vooral schrik hebben dat je door die anderen raar bevonden zal worden. Terwijl die angst in wezen zinloos is: je bent bang van iets dat zich in je eigen hoofd afspeelt, bang van verwachtingen die er misschien niet eens zijn. Dat kan verlammend werken. Bovendien bestaat raar helemaal niet, en indien wel, dan is iedereen raar.'

'Toch is het, denk ik, niet per se ongezond om angstig te zijn en je dienovereenkomstig te gedragen. Het zal wel een zelfverdedigingsmechanisme zijn, een menselijke reflex om niet uitgelachen of uitgesloten te worden. En wellicht is het voor de maatschappij ook beter als we op zijn minst proberen om een béétje normaal te doen.'

'Ik verdenk Liana Finck ervan hoogsensitief te zijn. Ze heeft in elk geval een hoge graad van zelfbewustz... biografisch

is heel rudimentair, bijna lelijk. Maar dat maakt het net echter: er zijn geen kladversies. De onbevangenheid waarmee ze existentiële vragen tegemoet treedt, vind ik erg verfrissend. Vaak zit ze er *boenk* op. Ik herken mezelf wel in haar manier

Johan Sebastiaan Stuer is dichter en cartoonist bij Humo en redacteur en nieuwslezer bij De ideale wereld.

SUNSET DOESN'T MEAN THAT WE LOSE THE SUN

RAISED BY WOLVES
SUGAR DADDY

WARGASM

ZIGGY

ECHO

PET JAGUAR

REALITY CRISIS

BLADE

WATCH TV

CREATE YOUR OWN IDOL

CUTTER

I'D LIKE TO BLOW UP THE WORLD

BOOM

it's only a story
it's not real
don't worry
there IS a happy
ENDING

SPIDER.

PLUG YOURSELF INTO THIS PLEASURE PORTAL, PLEASE.

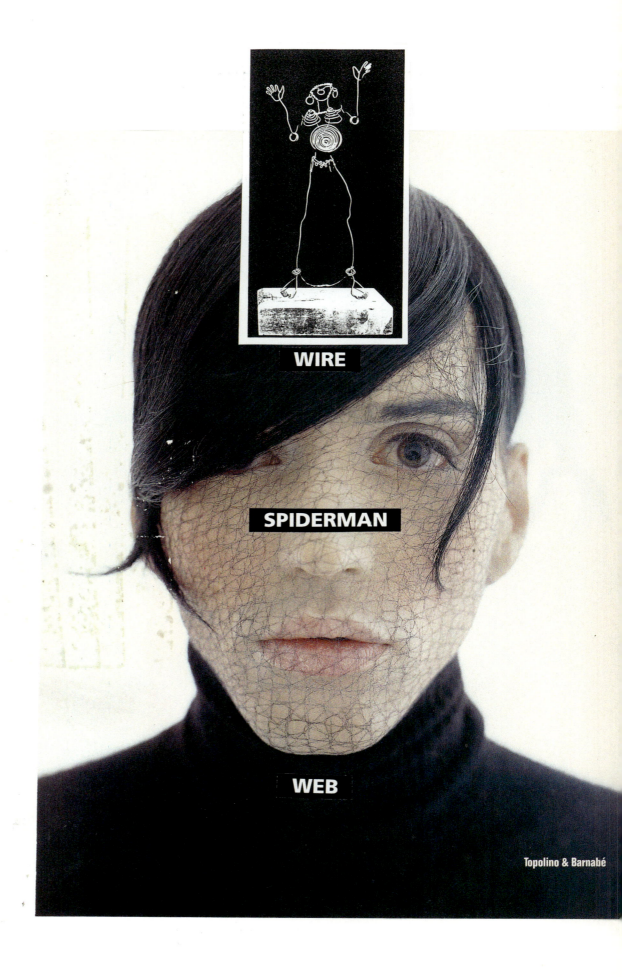

Topolino & Barnabé

DARE TO CREATE

Laced denim dress by Gucci; Denim patchwork boots by Louis Vuitton; Glass drop earring by Slim Barrett

ZODIAC STARS DANCE
WUNK *celestial bodies* SMILE
BATTERIES NOT INCLUDED

Ten westen van Stonehenge, 2 augustus 1995: een geavanceerde GSM?

De 'drievoudige halve maan' van East Meon. Als *u* dit gemaakt hebt, wil u dan uw vinger opsteken?

Het kosmisch ministerie van Ontwikkelingshulp heeft hard gewerkt in 1995. Deze prachtige cirkels hebben bijvoorbeeld een totale doorsnee van 123 meter.

Heilige geometrie: de 'Vector Equilibrium'. Als iemand hier iets mee bedoelt, wil die dan laten weten wàt?

Hierbij vindt u een staalkaart van wat onze verre vrienden zoal in hun picturale mars hebben. Dit is het zogenaamde 'vuurwiel' (juli 1995).

Dit patroon dook op in East Meon, *home of the* graancirkels.

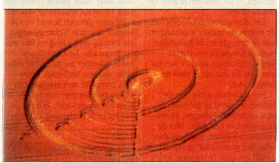
Zou dit de omloopbaan van een komeet voorstellen? En zo ja, wat heb dat voor nut?

De mooiste van wat sommigen 'de zonnesystemen' onder de graancirkels noemen.

... This is like a Frankenstein-like attitude, imbuing a man-made creation with life ...

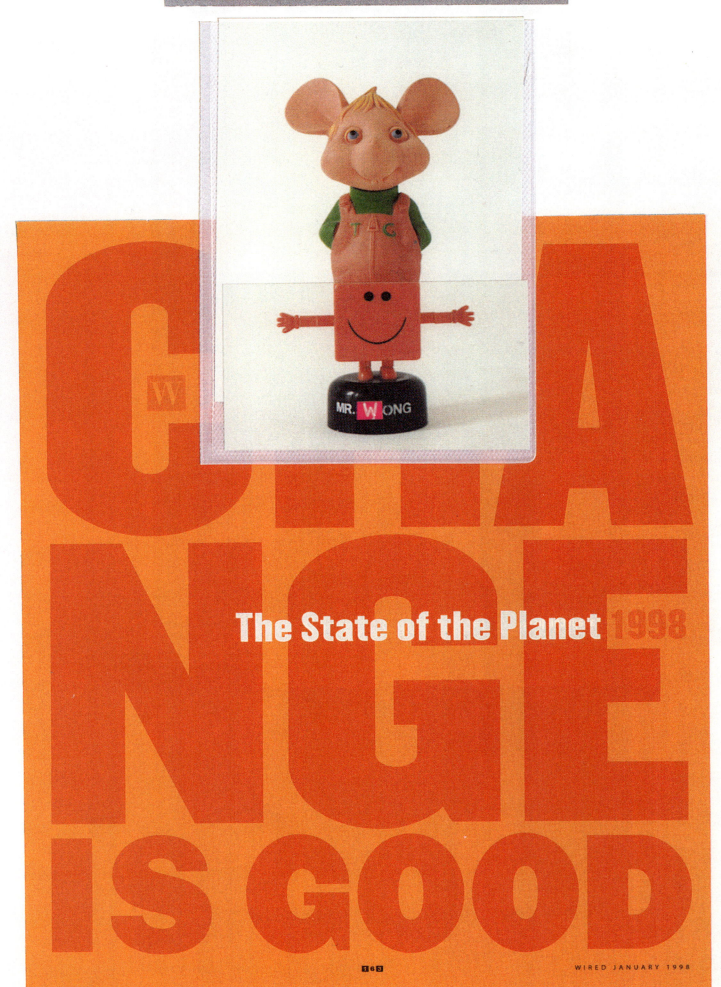

CHANGE IS GOOD

The State of the Planet 1998

WIRED JANUARY 1998

STOP TERRORIZING OUR WORLD

SILHOUETTE

PURE

BLOW-UP

GILBERT & GEORGE

DICK_HEAD

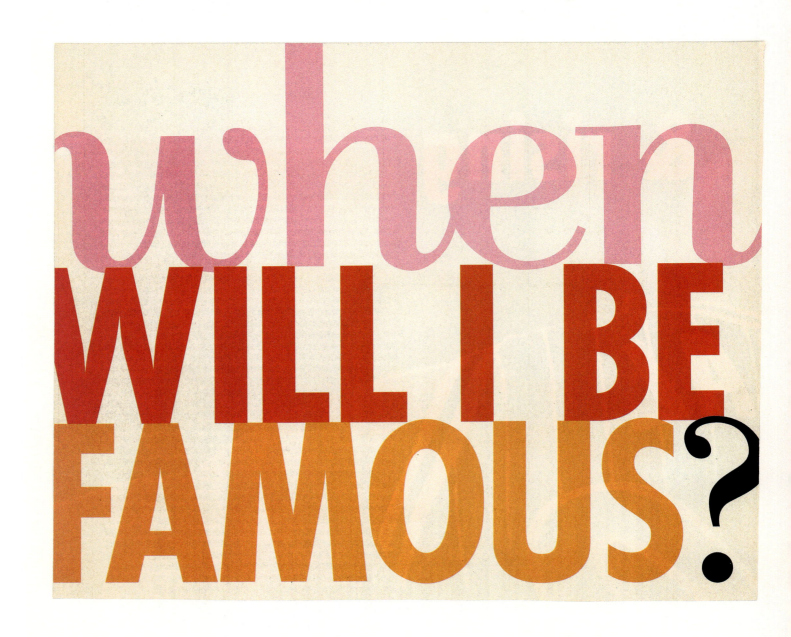

REACH INTO MY TUNNELS

«Tell me, who stole your smile»

drew
WILD
honey

«Tell me, who stole your smile»

Big
is strong

SUNSET DOESN'T MEAN THAT WE LOSE THE SUN *(repeated)*

Paulette wears Cutler And Gross glasses, £90, from Cutler And Gross, 16 Knightsbridge Green, London SW1; Ichi Ni San, 26 Bell Street, Glasgow and branches of Whistles nationwide. ● Vince wears glasses bought in America ● Sharon wears glasses, £10, from Souled Out, Unit 25, Portobello Green Arcade, 281 Portobello Road, London W10. ● Monica wears Cutler And Gross glasses, £56, as before.

It feels like a vibrator

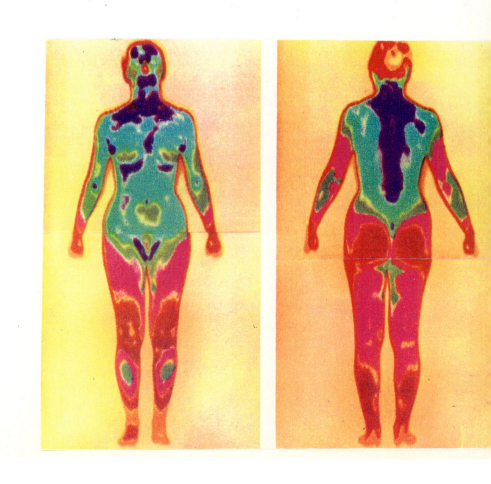

coming out of your

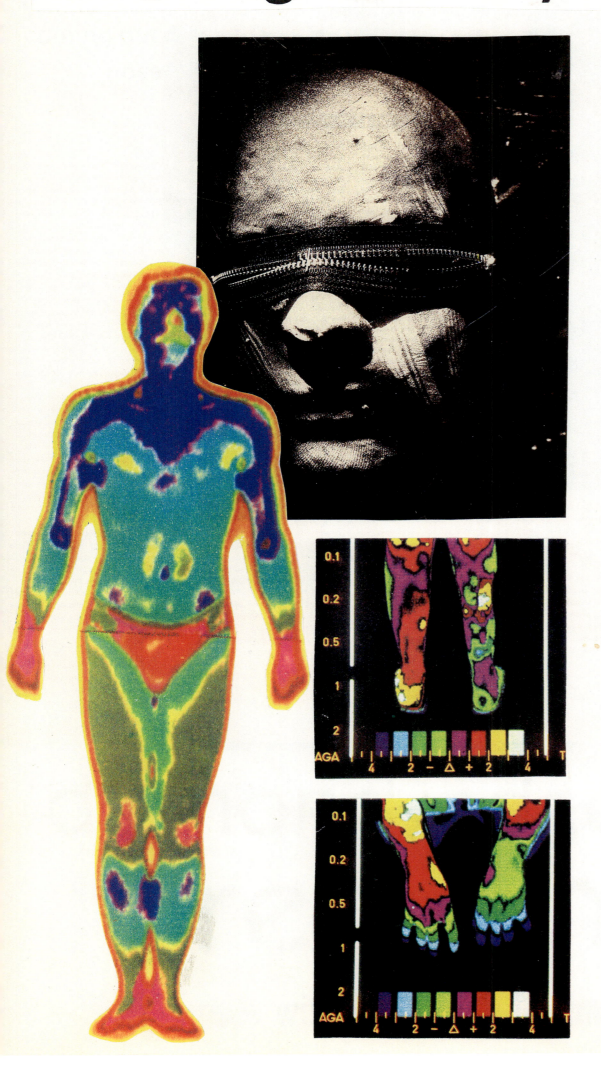

Colour is Power

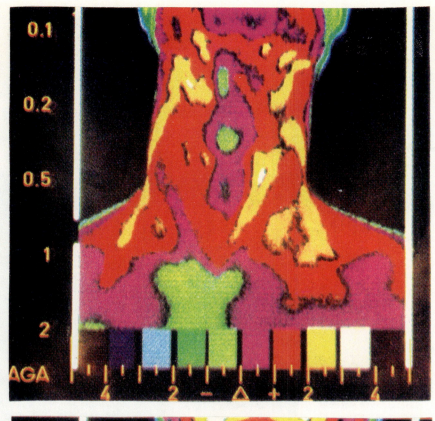
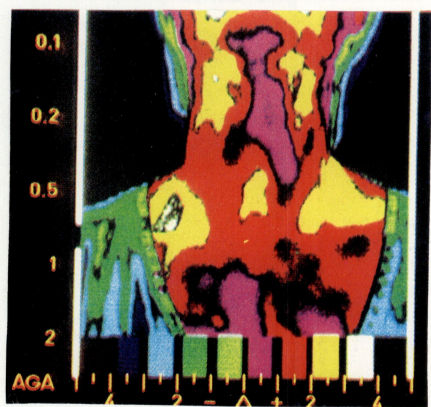

diamond-edged erection

"Your senses will never be the same!"

the bigger

WAITING
FOR
MR.
BIG

the better

BEAUTIFY
BIG

INHALT / CONTENT / CONTENU

SEITE / PAGE   THEMA / TOPIC / SUJET

ALL IS TRANSIENT
Together we are strong!"

DAWLEETOO!
LOST CITY OF Z W
WEIRD TALES
LOVECRAFT
THE CALL OF CTHULHU
WINCKLE PICKERS
MASTERPIECE
WHIPLASH

WARRIORS

INHALT / CONTENT / CONTENU

SEITE / PAGE THEMA / TOPIC / SUJET

SPACE, ENERGY & LIGHT
EXPERIMENTAL ELECTRONIC AND ACOUSTIC SOUNDSCAPES 1961-88

HERE MEN FROM THE PLANET EARTH
FIRST SET FOOT UPON THE MOON
JULY 1969, A. D.
WE CAME IN PEACE FOR ALL MANKIND

AND IF THE LIGHT SHOULD FALL ...
ON FUTURE INTERPLANETARY TRAVEL, THE SOUNDS OF SPACE SHALL CONTINUE TO ENTER THE SOUL FOR WITHIN THE DIMENSIONS OF THE NATURAL EARTH AND THE HUMAN BODY LIFE RESTS BALANCED IN THE FLOW OF WIND, THE PULSE OF THE HEART AND THE FRAGILITY OF THE PLANETS.

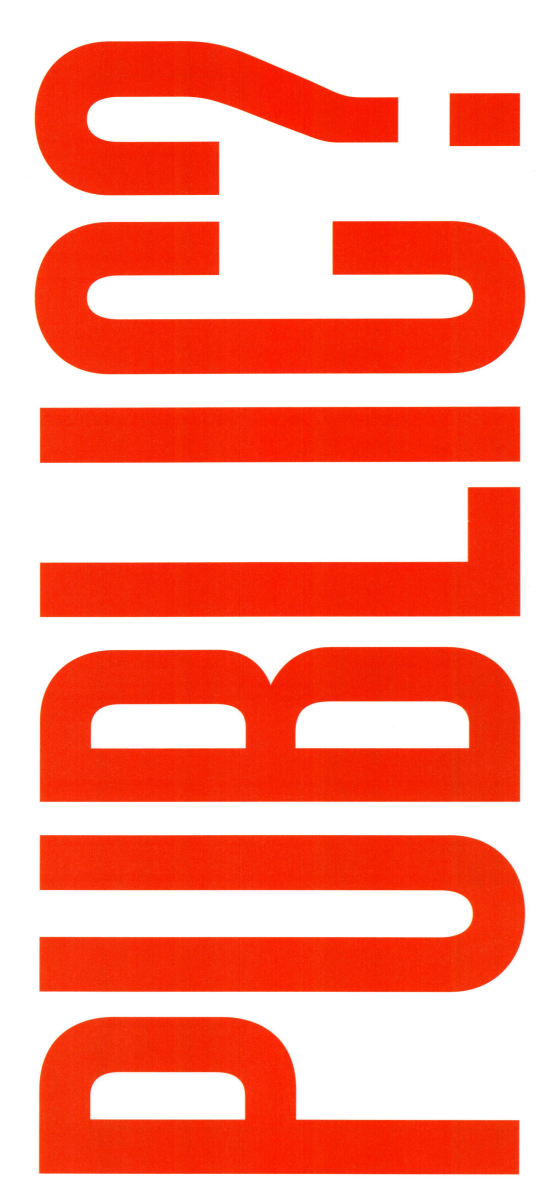

REBOOT
PROVOCATIVE
POWER

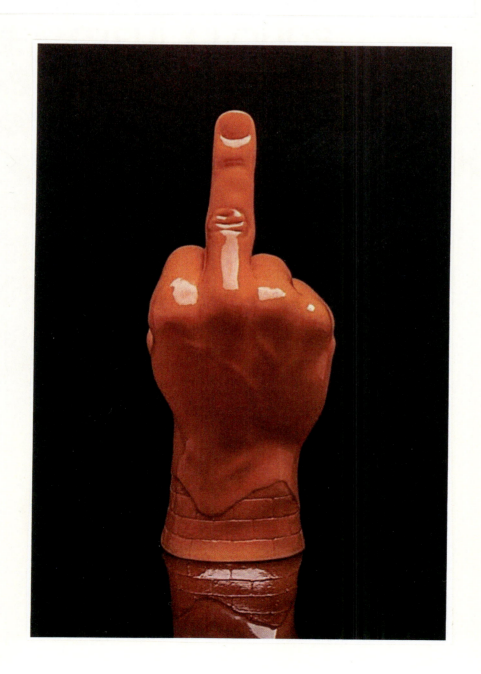

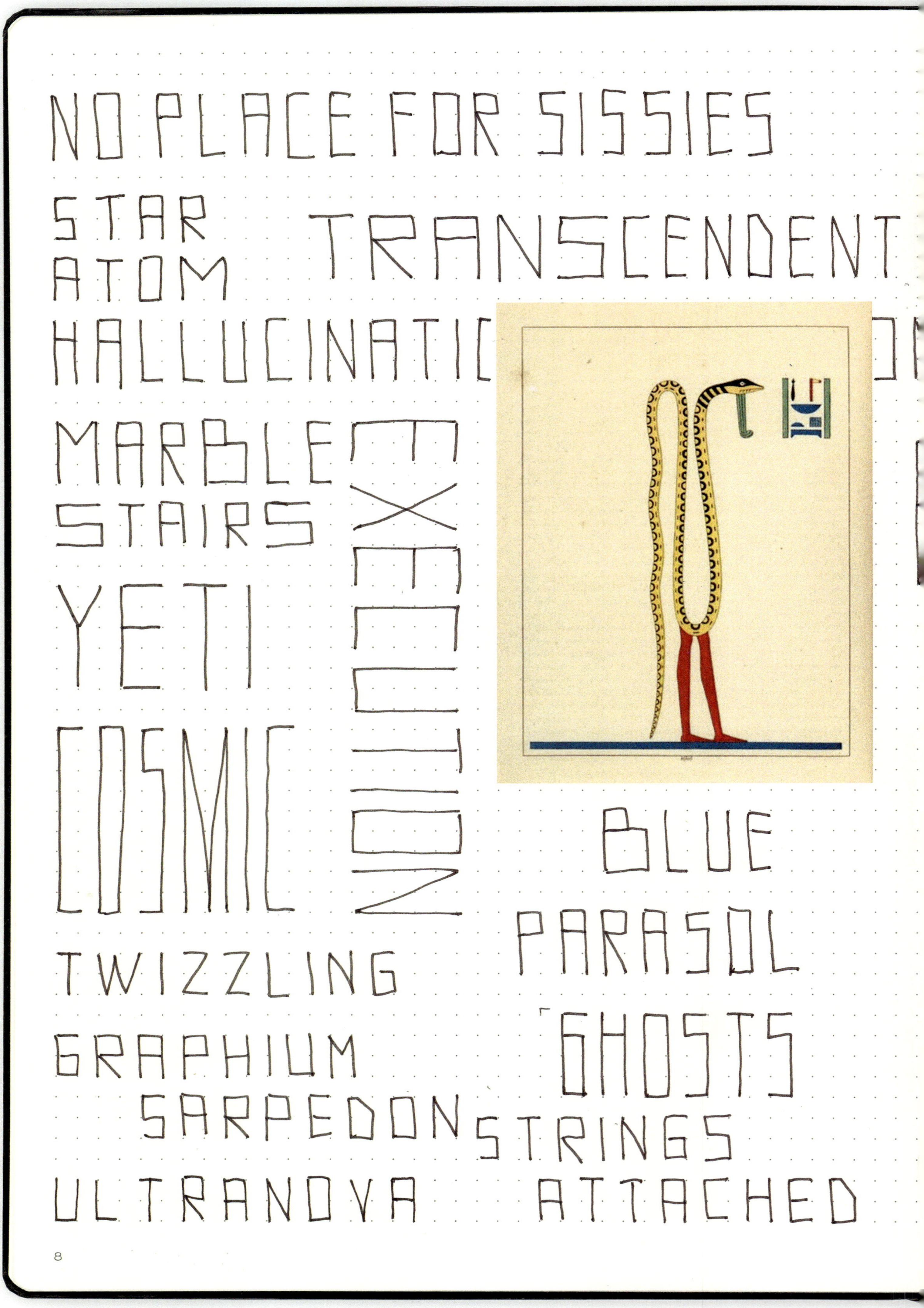

NO PLACE FOR SISSIES

STAR
ATOM
HALLUCINATION
MARBLE
STAIRS
YETI
COSMIC

TRANSCENDENT

EXECUTION

TWIZZLING
GRAPHIUM
SARPEDON
ULTRANOVA

BLUE
PARASOL
GHOSTS
STRINGS
ATTACHED

GLORIOUS
DISTORTION
CRASH
COMA
RACE

ECHO
WAR

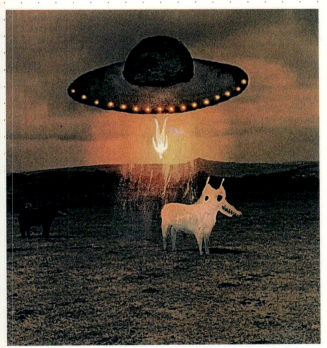

THE HEIGHTS

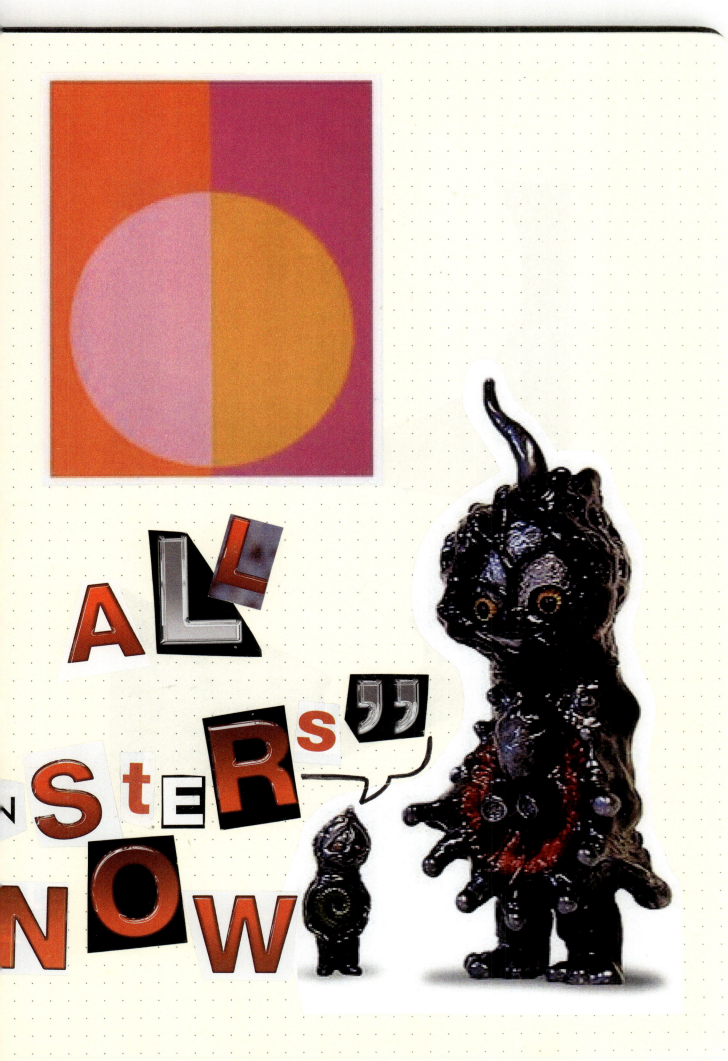

Killer instincts

FOTO JEAN PIERRE HORLIN/THE IMAGE BANK

**Tuin van de Thien Mu-pagode,
Hué, Vietnam**

BE
A
TRUE
ORIGINAL

NO FUTURE?

a chain
explosion of spiritual avant-garde ideology

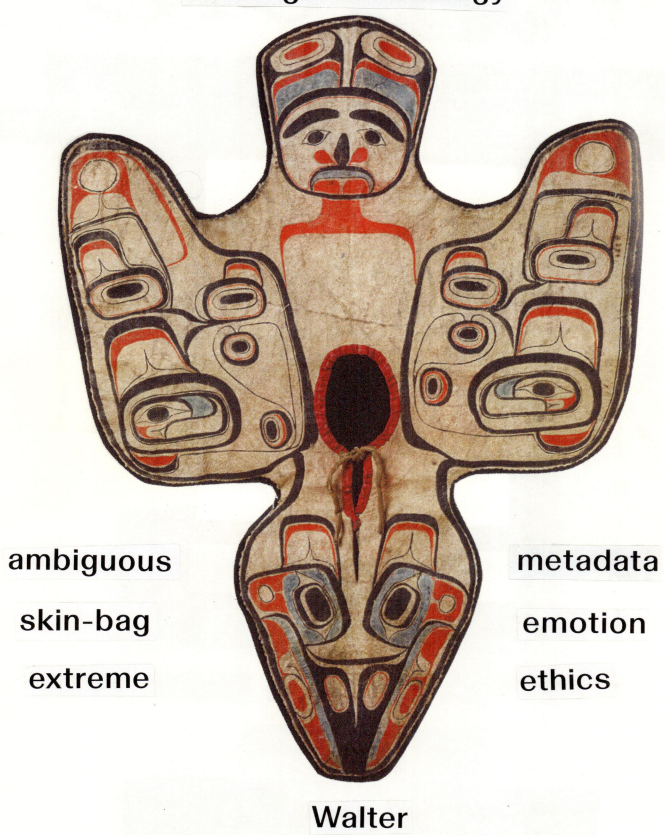

ambiguous

skin-bag

extreme

metadata

emotion

ethics

Walter

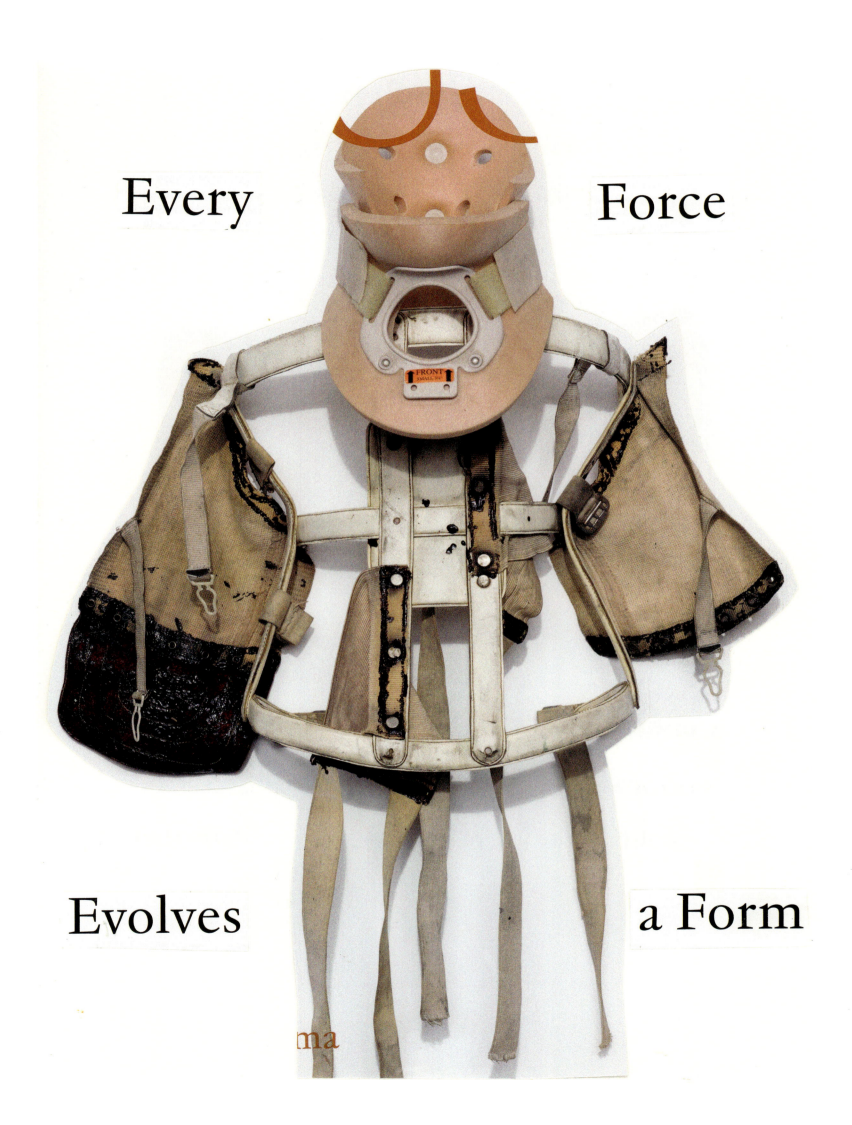

Every Force

Evolves a Form

KISS THE FUTURE!

COLOPHON

CONCEPT
Walter Van Beirendonck
Paul Boudens
Dominique Nzeyimana
for
Not Dead Yet projects

COLLAGES & CUT-OUTS
© Walter Van Beirendonck, 2024

GRAPHIC DESIGN
Paul Boudens

TEXT
Dominique Nzeyimana

IMAGE SELECTION
Walter Van Beirendonck
Paul Boudens

COVER IMAGES
© Walter Van Beirendonck, 2024

THANKS TO
Xavier Hufkens
Paul McCarthy
Ana Zoe Zijlstra

IMAGE SCANNING
Fotorama, Ghent, Belgium

IMAGE EDITING
Jeroen Lommelen

COPY-EDITING
Stefaan Pauwels
Derek Scoins

PROJECT MANAGEMENT
Hadewych Van den Bossche

PUBLISHER
Gautier Platteau

PRINTING & BINDING
Trento, Italy

ISBN 978 94 6494 138 8
D/2024/11922/46
NUR 452

HANNIBAL

© Hannibal Books, 2024

www.hannibalbooks.be

All rights reserved. No part of this publication may be reproduced or transmitted in any form or by any means, electronic or mechanical, including photocopy, recording or any other information storage and retrieval system, without prior permission in writing from the publisher.